D1606550

Strategic Brand Management
for B2B Markets

To
My Parents
Amma and Papa

Contents

I. Thinking about B2B Brands

II. Creating Corporate Brands: The Key Asset of any B2B Brand

III. Brand Communications

$ 21.28

1-3-12

YBP Firm

IV. Holistic Brand Management

V. The Future Challenges

List of Tables

Annexure Tables

List of Figures

Preface

Why This Book

The power of strong brands has either not been recognized or ignored by the marketers engaged in marketing of industrial goods and services. As a student of Business-to-Business (B2B) marketing for more than 40 years, I too feel strongly that the area of brands and brand management is either dormant or underleveraged. I think that the Indian perspective and context would supplement the attempts of the authors from developed economies—in the area of business markets—to fill this void. So the two primary purposes of this book are:

- To create intellectual capital rooted in the Indian context with Indian examples.
- To fill a glaring void in the field of B2B marketing. As admitted by several pundits like Professors Kotler and Keller (from the USA) and Consultants Hague and Jackson (from the UK), not much has been written on how to create powerful B2B brands.

The purpose of this book is not to become a substitute to several excellent books that are available in the areas of brands, brand management and advertisement management. Nor is it to become a professional guide to develop good advertising and promotional campaigns. But the purpose is to motivate the marketers deeply entrenched in B2B marketing to unleash the underleveraged power of brand to create competitive advantages for growth.

The Plan of the Book

This book is divided in five parts.

Part I contains three chapters and deals with thinking about brands. Collectively they provide a good feel and exposure of the brand and branding issues for B2B marketers.

Part II deals with the role and importance of the most strategic asset of any organization: the corporate brand. The three chapters in this part discuss the brands of Tata, Larsen & Toubro (L&T) and Infosys. Readers would benefit and feel inspired with these three excellent stories of corporate India.

Part III deals with brand communications: the nuts-and-bolts issues in brand building. They too are critical in brand management. Efficient management of the 'small spends' on the communications elements will go a long way in contributing to the creation of a strong brand. Recognizing the importance of the Internet and websites, a separate chapter has been dedicated to the effective management of websites.

Part IV is based on holistic brand management. This, as brand pundits claim, is the core idea of creating and sustaining strong brands. Six cases of B2B brands included here are: Sintex, Motor Starter Type MK1 of L&T, Tata Steel's Structura brand for steel tubes, L&T Eutectic, OTIS Elevators in India and Elgi Equipments—an air compressor company. Collectively the cases provide a variety of perspective and help readers grasp the point that brand is much more than having just a communication programme.

Part V discusses future challenges of B2B brands. I have identified the creation of global brands as a very important challenge for the future Indian B2B marketers. Today there exists a very wide gap between the global and Indian B2B brands. The challenges would demand global competitiveness, global awareness and global recognition. The B2B marketers from India need to reorient their entire effort to recast themselves in order to play in the global market arena. There is a separate chapter on rekindling the aspiration through the idea of brand. It is directed at the millions of unknown B2B marketers. This chapter serves my key passion of urging the lesser known B2B marketers to dream and become big brands and great companies. The last chapter of this part is a reflection on brand mystique, and is followed by closing suggestions.

Who Could Be the Target Audience for This Book?

- Managers from both developed and developing economies engaged in business brands.
- Entrepreneurs belonging to small and medium enterprises.
- Students opting for specialized course in B2B markets both in India and abroad.
- Students in brand management wanting to expand their horizon to know and understand the challenges of creating B2B brands in contrast to Business-to-Consumer (B2C) markets.

At 12 noon, on 24 November 2009, a click on google.com for all articles and books on brands resulted in 42 million hits. A second click for all articles and books on B2B brands indicated only 55,500 hits. The gap is too wide and glaring. Looking at its economic importance, the world of B2B and brands deserves, if not 40 million, at least a million-plus search results. I am hopeful that this book will fill this void.

Acknowledgements

This book would not have been possible without the support of many individuals and organizations. Though it would be difficult to mention all, some individuals deserve special acknowledgement. First and foremost is the support of the Director, Fr. Abraham of Xavier Labour Relations Institute (XLRI), Jamshedpur who gladly and promptly provided all the required support for my research. I am grateful to him as well as XLRI.

A set of individuals whose writings and presentations helped in expanding and strengthening my knowledge and conceptual base in the area of B2B brands are: Kotler and Pfoertsch; Kevin Lane Keller; Hague and Jackson; Narayana Murthy (Founder and mentor, Infosys); Muthuraman (ex-Managing Director or MD, Tata Steel); Gopalakrishnan (Executive Director, Tata Sons) and Rama Bijapurkar(a leading brand guru of India). I wish to thank them.

In the early phases of my research, I had interacted with several directors and senior executives. These include: Mr B.K. Jhawar (CMD, Usha Martin Group); Mr C.D. Kamath (ex-MD, Tata Refractories Limited); Mr B.L. Raina (ex-MD, Tinplate Company of India); Mr Rana Sinha (MD, Telcon Ltd); Dr Jairam Varadaraj (MD, Elgi Group); Mr Anand Sen (Vice President or VP, Flat Products of Tata Steel); Mr Vivek Kamra (Executive-in-Charge, Tubes Division); Mr Anurag Behar (MD, Wipro Hydraulic Systems) and Mr Aditya Jha (AVP, Corporate Marketing, Infosys Limited). Thank you all for your time and insights.

The L&T Group, starting from Mr A.M. Naik (CMD), several directors and a large team of senior- and middle-level managers deserve a special mention for sharing their views. This helped me in developing the chapter on Corporate Brand for L&T. Mr K.R. Palta (Senior Executive, VP, L&T), based in Delhi, deserves a special mention in setting the tone for my data collection activities within L&T. Mr R.N. Mukhija (Director, L&T) and his team of senior executives of Switchgear division spared time to develop a case on Switchgear Standard Products Group. It was a very substantial effort to co-ordinate interviews within L&T. Deepak Morada (General Manager, Corporate Communication), provided excellent support. He and his team provided information on brand-building activities of L&T. The transparency and enthusiasm demonstrated by the L&T team speaks volumes about the greatness of this organization.

I wish to acknowledge the influence of Dr J.J. Irani (Director, Tata Sons and ex-MD, Tata Steel) on my thinking in several areas related to managing businesses. My long association with him has enabled me to know and understand many facets of the house of the Tatas. Mr Gopalakrishnan (Executive Director, Tata Sons and the main architect of brand-building initiatives of the house of Tatas), was gracious enough to provide time to share his deeper thoughts and highly refined ideas. My thanks are also extended to him.

A special mention is also due to the team of young managers from Tata Steel. These include Ms Atrayee Sarkar, Mr Piyush Gupta, Rajiv Singhal of Long Products Group and Ashish Anupam and Shenoy from Tubes Division. They were prompt and enthusiastic to share their views and information. Sanjay Chaudhari (Head, Corporate Affairs and Communications), was more than willing to share as to how Tata Steel and the house of Tatas have geared up for brand building and communicating with the stakeholders. My special thanks to Sanjay and his team.

The contribution of the Telcon team under Rana Sinha, MD, is similar to that of the young executives of Tata Steel. The team spared time to interact with me twice in Bangalore. Their enthusiasm to share unique branding challenges of Telcon was very informative. I am grateful to them for their time and transparency in sharing the issues.

Ms Sarita of Jasubhai Group needs a special mention for sharing her views on branding elements and their role in creating strong B2B brands.

Two close friends from my alma mater, Indian Institute of Management, Ahmedabad, deserve special mention. One is my class fellow and close friend Mr S.B. Dangayach (Danga), MD, Sintex, Industries Ltd, who kept on encouraging me to complete the book. Danga not only motivated me but also provided all possible help to develop the case on Sintex. The other is Mr Madan Mohanka, CMD, Tega Group of Industries, a hardcore B2B organization. Madan was always available with his suggestions and views. My special thanks to both of them.

Sanchita, my research associate, was an excellent and efficient support for data mining and its analysis. My secretary Treasa's support came very handy in patient typing and re-typing the drafts. A big thank you to you both.

The team of SAGE Publications, including the sales and editorial staff, were the major motivators. Though very late to publish a book, the team never gave up and maintained the follow-up. Many thanks for the interest.

Besides the support from outsiders, the most powerful and a 24-hour support ever since I conceived the idea of developing a book on B2B brands has been Mani, my wife. Words would fail to indicate the importance of her role and support. On one hand she helped me in creating the folders of various chapters, visiting thousands of websites, collection of references and typing and re-typing of innumerable drafts on the laptop and on the other she kept my morale high by mentoring and motivating me throughout the period of two years. By forcing me to remain focused in this project, she brought in a lot of discipline that was required in the completion of the book. Our children and grandchildren, who have been away from Jamshedpur, were closely monitoring the progress. They have been anxiously waiting for me to finish the book. My very affectionate thanks to them for keeping my morale high and reminding me that 'I too can do it!'

Thinking about B2B Brands

1

With our thoughts we make the world.

—Gautam Buddha

*A man is but the product of his thoughts,
what he thinks, he becomes.*

—Mahatma Gandhi

*One of the greatest pieces of economic wisdom
is to know what you do not know.*

—John Kenneth Galbraith

1

Brands and B2B Markets: Putting Things in Perspective

> There is one asset, an intangible one, that stands head and shoulders above all the others and that cannot be easily outsourced: the brand.
>
> —Bedbury 2002

> Brands differentiate, reduce risk and complexity and communicate the benefits and value a product or service can provide. This is just as true in B2B as it is in B2C.
>
> —Kotler and Pfoertsch 2006

Idea of Brand is Widely Known

It is my belief that amongst the long list of marketing concepts and jargons, brand would perhaps be the most widely known to both professionals and novices. From several platforms, I share an experience to support this belief. The situation was a training programme of 35 fresh and young trainees with no idea of either business or marketing. I began my class by asking as to what comes to their minds when they hear the word 'brand'. Their answers baffled and impressed me a great deal. Within 30 minutes of thinking aloud, the group covered all the aspects of brand management beginning from brand loyalty and ending with the gains from strong brand equity. They shared that brand differentiates and enables a marketer to earn premium. They observed that brand is a consistent delivery of the promise. Besides sharing the idea of top of the mind recall, they also shared that brand reduces the risk for the customer in buying decisions. They went on to share the idea of brands lending status to its owner and the user of the brand. In short, they shared all that has seemingly been written by thousands of authors in millions of articles.

So if the idea is so widely known, why does it need to be re-written, specifically for the B2B marketers. The answer is simple. Knowledge is different from practice.

It is the purpose of this book to convince the millions of B2B marketers that no matter what your market is—crane or crank shaft (an auto component)—the idea of brand is useful. In this chapter, I would like to share views, anecdotes and experiences to create a proper perspective for the readers to understand the challenges in managing brand driven businesses.

We are Living in a Branded World and This would Continue

Brand pundits say we live in a branded world. Jack Trout shares that 'there are more than 2.5 million registered trademarks in the United States alone and at least 3 million more in the rest of the world. Last year more than 500,000 new names were registered around the world' (Trout 2009). Without brands, life would have been drab and difficult. As Keller (2008: 24) says:

> In our increasingly complex world, all of us as individuals and business managers, face more choices to make with less time. Thus a strong brand's ability to simplify consumer decision making, reduce risk and set expectations is invaluable. Creating strong brands that deliver on that promise, and maintaining and enhancing the strength of those brands over time, is a management imperative.

Table 1.1 provides a consolidated view of brand and branding benefits of some experts.

Table 1.1 Books and Articles Identify Several Payoffs from Strong Brands

Keller (2008: 29) Role that brands play	Anderson and Narus (2003: 156)	Kotler and Pfoertsch (2006: 47)	Hague and Jackson (1994: 54)
For consumers • Identification of the source of the product • Assignment of responsibility to product maker • Risk reducer • Promise, bond or pact with maker or product • Symbolic device • Signal of quality For Manufacturers • Means of identification to simplify handling or tracing • Means of legally protecting unique features • Signal of quality level to satisfied customers • Means of endowing products with unique associations • Source of competitive advantage • Source of financial returns	• Greater willingness to sample or trial of the offering • Reduction in time to close the sale of the offering • Greater likelihood of purchasing the offering • Willingness to award a large share of purchase requirement • Willingness to pay a higher price • Greater unwillingness to switch to competitor offerings after price increases • Less willingness to sample or trial competitor offerings	• Increase information efficiency • Risk reduction • Value added/image benefit creation • Create brand loyalty • Differentiate marketing efforts • Create preferences • Command price premium • Create brand image • Increase sales	• Brands give status • Brands make it easy to buy • Brands block out all others • Brands make buying safe • Using brands for joint ventures and licencing • Using brands for pulling demand downstream

In India, Muthuraman, MD of Tata Steel (2001–09) seems to have grasped this scope and payoffs of strong brands way ahead of Tata Steel's competitors. He observed:

> Anything can be branded if it is worthwhile. I see no reason why steel should not be branded. When you see a soap selling at a price higher than other soaps, for reasons which are not obvious and non complex, I do not see why one steel company should not sell at a higher price than other steel, especially if it deserves it. (Ravikumar 2006)

Elsewhere Muthuraman has been quoted:

> If the brand is positioned and developed, it will create a segment in the market that is loyal to the brand and what it stands for. This will offset the uncertainties brought about by that segment of customers which buys products only on price considerations. The loyal customer is able to build a stable relationship with the brand, and thus reduce the vagaries of price for the supplier, while assuring the customer a good product. Branding a product synergizes with the company's brand image. The economic benefits of branding lie in the protection of its price lines as well as of the company's market capitalization. Branding becomes necessary in the steel business because of the variety of steels that are available (around 20,000). The steel used in an auto rickshaw differs *from* that used in a car, and *from* car to car. The steel made by different companies can also differ for the same specifications. The variety can cause confusion in the mind of the consumer. (XLRI 2003)

So if steel can be branded, why cannot the other products be branded too? And if it took 100 years for Tata Steel to realize the hidden potential of branding steel, then it should not be late for any other B2B marketer, big or small. Box 1.1 provides the meaning of brand as defined by the American Marketing Association.

Box 1.1   The Meaning of Brand and Branding

According to the American Marketing Association (AMA), a *brand* is a 'name, term, sign, symbol, or design, or a combination of them, intended to identify the goods and services of one seller or group of sellers and to differentiate them from those of competition'. Technically speaking then, whenever a marketer creates a new name, logo, or symbol for a new product, he or she has created a brand.

Source: Keller (1998: 24).

Even B2B Customers Prefer Brands

Muthuraman and Tata Steel are seemingly not branding their products for the sake of branding. There is enough evidence to claim that even B2B buyers prefer to buy branded products. Consider the following two instances.

Vishal is the CEO of an organization which is in the business of producing copper wires. These are used by the electrical industry such as those dealing in motors, transformers, fans, home appliances and other end uses. His organization's sales turnover in the year 2008 was around Rs 2,000 million (US\$ 40 million). It employs around 8–10 professionals and 200 workers. In several ways, it is a one-man show. Besides copper rods, which account for nearly 85 per cent of his annual purchase (copper rods is the raw material for Vishal's organization), his annual buying for other purchases could be around Rs 200 million (US\$ 4 million). This includes capital equipments, maintenance and repair components and several consumables and electrical and mechanical items. When asked about his views on buying branded products, his prompt response was: 'I prefer to buy only the branded products. The reason—brands assure quality and consistency. If I had ways and means to measure the performance, I could have opted to buy the "non-branded" products. Unfortunately, that is neither practical nor desirable.' Like Vishal, there would be millions of small and medium enterprises (SMEs) in B2B marketing in India (as of 2008, India had around 2 million SMEs [CMIE 2009]) managing business in the similar manner for their organizational buying. To Vishal, the second question was, whether brand has any role for his products, i.e., copper wires. The prompt observation was an emphatic 'Yes'. He shared that the leaders in his industry get premium as they enjoy superior brand image due to better service and consistency in quality.

We may argue that with limited resources, these B2B customers are resorting to buying the brands. This may not be the truth for large B2B customers with substantial resources and expertise for buying. So now consider the case of a giant steel producer of India. When asked about his views of buying branded products for his organization, the head of purchasing shared that against the total buying value of nearly Rs 80,000 million (US$ 1,600 million) for FY 2008–09, 95 per cent would be of branded products. His organization prefers brands for superior performance. For most of these, it fixes the prices based on annual rate contracts. The evaluation includes the total cost of product plus service. He went on to explain that in many cases the initial price may be high, but the total cost of owning and using these turn out to be low. In his excitement to claim the preference for branded products, he shared that even for a product like coal, his organization pays a premium when it specifies a particular mine in Australia. Within minutes he rattled a long list of companies and their products. His narration went on as follows:

> For electrical, the sources are ABB, Siemens and L&T. For bearings the brands preferred are SKF, FAG and NSK. For gears we prefer Shanti Gears. For a product like idlers and rollers used in the conveyor belts we buy from TRF. For pumps, the suppliers could be KSB and Kirloskar. For office equipments, we prefer to buy from Godrej.

For printers, the preference is for HP. For desktops computers, it is either IBM or HP. For Copier it is either Xerox, or Canon. For software services it is IBM, Oracle or SAP. For IT service related products, his organization gives emphasis on the sources who invest heavily in R&D. (Thus as he shared SAP has an R&D set up in Dusseldorf where they have employed more than 9,000 people in Germany and this has influenced the decision to prefer SAP.) For water treatment chemicals the choice is GE. For wire ropes—it prefers Usha Martin—UMI—and for compressors Atlas Copco and Elgi Equipment. For a consumable like refractories, TRL (Tata Refractories Limited) is the first preference. For specialty lubricants and grease, Indian Oil Corporation (IOC) and Balmer Lawrie is its preference. For machine tools it prefers Skoda and HMT. For large and very expensive capital equipment like blast furnaces, hot rolling mills, and so on, it prefers equipment from Germany or Japan. For awarding civil and construction contracts L&T (ECC) stands out to be its preference.

He took three to four minutes to rattle out what came to him first—something like a 'top of mind' recall. After a deep breath, he mentioned the list would run into thousands.

Summing up the experience of two ends of a spectrum—an SME and a big B2B customer—one can safely make the following statement: 'Brands are balms for assurance and peace of mind for a large number of B2B customers.'

Buying without Specifying the Specifications: The Ultimate Power of a Strong Brand

But to me, the ultimate reward of a strong brand is when the B2B buyers do not waste time in writing the specifications and inviting competitive bids and then spend time in evaluation before placement of the orders. In today's competitive environment where selecting between several similar choices has become a major headache even for the organizational buyer, the B2B marketer has established an emotional connect with the customers. This outcome is in line with what Kotler and Pfoertsch share: 'While reasons do lead us to conclusions, emotions are the ones which leads us to action' (Kotler and Pfoertsch 2006: 58). By opting for strong brands, Dhirubhai, the legendry founder of Reliance, seems to have created very large and complex projects in record time. Here is one example of relationships between Reliance and L&T that led to the creation of a Petro Chemical Complex at Patalganga near Mumbai.[1] Box 1.2 provides the details.

Box 1.2   L&T (ECC) and Reliance Industries

Around 1982, the then head of ECC, the construction division of L&T, and his chief engineer met the legendary founder of Reliance Industries Limited (RIL)—the largest private sector organization of India. The meeting was at the request of Dhirubhai—the creator of Reliance. He was then setting up RIL's first petrochemical complex in Patalganga near Navi Mumbai. Pointing at the pile of drawings from DuPont of the US (RIL's collaborators), Dhirubhai shared that his plant would be a 100 per cent replica of the DuPont plant. Against 22 months of DuPont, Dhirubhai was keen to commission the plant in 18 months. Early completion, as he shared, would help him to repay the money he had borrowed. ECC executives, though willing to construct the plant, expressed that before committing anything, ECC would like to study the drawings and

(Box 1.2 Continued)

(*Box 1.2 Continued*)

submit the proposal for time and money. How much time was needed to submit the proposal was the question asked by Dhirubhai. The response of the Chief Engineer of ECC was three months. To this, Dhirubhai's prompt response was to take these three months to submit the proposal, but the execution time would then be 15 months, i.e., three months less from the total of 18 months. This led to a discussion between the two executives in a separate room where the Director-in-Charge checked with the Chief Engineer regarding ECC's profit expectation. The Chief Engineer observed that a return of x per cent[2] could be a good return. After some deliberations both felt the cost plus approach could be the only way to start the project without any proposal. Apprehending that Dhirubhai may negotiate for some discount, they decided to quote for a little higher than their normal return. When asked to share what they have in mind, the Director mentioned: 'ECC would be willing to undertake the contract at cost plus basis. The payment could be made after it has been approved by the auditors.' 'What is this plus,' asked Dhirubhai. They answered: x+delta per cent. 'Done,' was the immediate response. The rest is history. The Patalganga project of RIL was completed in a record time of 18 months.

This awed and surprised DuPont a great deal. Reliance created a world record of completing a project of this size in 18 months. Later ECC helped Reliance set up the largest single location refinery of the world in Jamnagar in a record time of 36 months. It mobilized more than 10,000 workers on site.

Note: For reasons of confidentiality, I have not provided the actual figures.

Experience is Perception: But It is in Your Hand to Create the Perception

In its simplest form, the idea of 'brand' is meant for the purpose of identifying a product or service. Thus, an engine oil is named Castrol, a limestone is named Bulldog, a plastic water tank is named Sintex, a mild steel rod for construction of houses is named TISCON, a ceiling fan is named Khaitan, a plastic drum is known as Hastee, a plywood is named Kitply or an adhesive is named Fevicol. But then what is used as a name for identification starts acquiring an image and perception in the minds of the customers. This perception or image over a period of time gets affected by several experiences of the customers. Soon these images become sticky or permanent in the minds of customers. We then start hearing feedbacks like

TISCON is good or bad, Sintex is good or bad, and so on. These customer experiences do not remain confined to product quality alone. They are also formed on the basis of buying experiences, quality of service and honesty and integrity of the marketer. Soon we start hearing words like reputation, trustworthiness and honesty of a marketer. 'He would never let us down,' implies that product quality would be as per specification and as promised. Pricing would be fair, service would be prompt and if something goes wrong with the product, the marker would be willing to replace or repair the product. Soon the marketer may earn reputation of being trustworthy—*bharosemand*, Hindi word for being trustworthy. Marketers' claims such as 'Satisfaction guaranteed', 'Money back—No question asked' or 'We would replace the worn out part within 48 hours during warranty period no matter where the equipment is in the world, otherwise liquidity damages would be to our account' create images and perceptions in the mind. And if the experience is good, i.e., if the marketer abides by the promise, he would earn a positive word-of-mouth of 'promise delivered' or promise backed-up performance. A consistency in delivery of promise thus leads to the creation of a good and positive image. This image then becomes a 'brand'. A poor performance starts having a negative rub-off on the image of a brand. We then start hearing words like, in case of airlines, 'They are never on time', 'Their in-flight service is poor' or 'No matter what time of the day you try, their toll free numbers never work or you keep following instructions only to be told after half an hour of effort, that you did not exercise the right option—We are sorry!'

The world is full of such experiences. They are happening all the time in both B2C and B2B market spaces. These are the experiences which finally get reflected in the making of your company's brand. But, by now, one should be able to grasp the point that I am trying to make—your 'image building' is in your hands. If you want you can build a strong, positive image. This requires sustained efforts on all fronts—quality; service; commercial terms and behaviour. Linked with perception, brand is the ultimate reality for an organization. No matter what one does, perceptions are formed. Even for a large majority of hardcore B2B marketers—where visibility is nil to low to small customer base, may be 1 to 10—there would be perceptions; be it amongst bankers, suppliers, customers or employees. It is in your hands to manage and control these perceptions. The moment you want to manage perception, thinking about youself as a brand would help. It is your choice and your wish.

Everything Can be Branded: From Crane to Crankshaft

Brands, to begin with, are needed for the purpose of identification. The brand name helps marketers and buyers identify and specify the products. DuPont, a leading global player in chemicals, has 2,000 products and 1,500 brands (Keller 1998: 290). Similarly, Reliance Industries, a company dealing in petrochemical business, has more than 40 brands (RIL 2007–08). DuPont and Reliance are giants. But even a mid-size company like Tata Refractories Limited (TRL) marketing refractories, which are used to line steel vessels and furnaces and then bought as consumables, has more then 80 products under it. TRL is very proud of the brand loyalty its products command. The customers are willing to pay premium for these brands and competitors are keen to copy them. Likewise, Tata Steel has at least eight brands. Telcon, an earth moving equipment manufacturing company, similar to Caterpillar, has more than 20 sub-brands under its umbrella.

Brand or Get Branded

Let me relate the story of Danapur and Dalpat. In 2009, Dalpat was around 65 years old. Since the last 45 years he has been doing the cane and plastic gutting of chairs and sofa sets of XLRI, a well-known business management school of India. Besides XLRI, Dalpat, from time-to-time, also provides his services to the residents at the XLRI campus. Having stayed in campus for the last 33 years, I have used Dalpat's services several times. Since the last five years,

I have noticed that the 'guts' being used by Dalpat have not been lasting long. Earlier the guts of our garden chairs would last for at least two-and-a-half to three years. But over the last five years, the average life of these had reduced to one to one-and-a-half years. When probed regarding the same, Dalpat responded promptly: 'Earlier I used to use Danapur guts. Now they are not available. Being of superior quality, they lasted long. Now I am using the "Delhi" guts which are of poor quality.' Dalpat has no idea of the manufacturers and marketers at Danapur (a place in Bihar) or Delhi. Perhaps, retailers in Jamshedpur are selling these guts under the name from where they are receiving these, Danapur and Delhi. They are using the source identity to distinguish the two types of quality. Like others, Dalpat also did not know whether it was a lone manufacturer or were there several manufacturers of the guts he used in Danapur.

Some of you must be aware that plastic guts are made by tiny and small sector players belonging to the plastic processing industry. Their numbers may be more than 20,000 (as of 2009) in India (CMIE 2009). A large majority is unknown entities to the end customers. Similarly, their products are near commodities, i.e., where there is no scope for providing perceived differentiation by varying attributes and use of superior design, etc. Majority use the same raw material, similar machines and processing technology. For both B2B and B2C customers, price would be the sole criterion for buying. Most of these plastic products, being low priced, are also low involvement products, implying low buying efforts. But low involvement does not mean acceptance of sub-standard quality. Even when customers do not show any preference of brand for their first purchase, they soon, like in my case of 'gutting' of the garden chairs, become aware of several things about the product. Even for incidents which occur once in every two years, experience gets formed, and the image remains in the mind. Over a period of time 'source' becomes the means to discriminate even in case of buying of commodities. This is the beginning of branding. This awareness and good experience has created 'brand equity' for Danapur guts—an unknown entity in the minds of customers like Dalpat and me.

Even when marketers do not name and sell their products as 'generic products', customers like Dalpat would always create a means to distinguish and discern.

Brand is Built by 40,000 People, Branding is by 21: Understanding the Difference between Brand and Branding

L&T's Corporate Communications division employs 21 executives. It has been this way for more than 40 years. The division also has an advertising agency. These 21 people take care of all the branding issues of L&T from developing brochures to participation in trade fairs, media relations, internal communications and management of one common website to releasing advertisement for recruitments. In 2009, L&T employed 40,000 people. Its 75 business divisions and 40,000 people have been continuously maintaining high performance to ensure a strong brand image of L&T.

Reflecting on the brand-building initiatives of Tatas, Gopalakrishnan, Executive Director, Tata Sons, and the main architect of the brand-building initiatives of the house of Tatas, is making a similar point when he wants people to understand an important distinction between brand and branding. He shares that:

> The building of the Tata brand is different from the brand building of Tata. This is not a mere play of words; it is an important distinction. The building of the Tata Brand has been going on for 100 years. All that we have been humbly seeking to do, since 1999, is to employ tested brand-building techniques. Tata is a gigantic property; we are merely managing the brand, tracking it through organized research, and constantly refreshing and updating it. (Agrawal 2007)

As suggested by Kotler and Keller (2006: 275):

> Branding is endowing products and services with the power of a brand. Branding is all about creating the differences. Building a strong brand requires careful planning and a great deal of long term investment. At the heart of a successful brand is a great product or service, backed by creatively designed and executed marketing.

Brands cannot exist in vacuum. It would be foolish to think that fancy communication and promotional activities is all that is needed to achieve sales and a good brand image. To be a strong brand a firm has to score high on all the performance parameters. In order to remain competitive and a strong brand, Tata Steel invested over Rs 89 billion (Jagannathan 2002) between 1983 and 2001 in its modernization and expansion programmes. Besides capital expenditure, Tata Steel, through a series of several process improvements, became the lowest cost producer in the world by 2001. All these initiatives create a strong brand. Seemingly Tata Steel has done what Hague and Jackson (1994: xiii) have suggested: Branding may increase the success of a product but, without continual maintenance of quality standards and continuous search for improvement, the foundations are built on sand and long-term failure is assured.

In contrast to consumer product situations, the branding opportunities are limited for B2B marketers. This gets reflected in the low advertising budget for majority of B2B marketers. (see Chapter 7 for detailed discussions). However the low expenses on brand building should not lead to the conclusion that brand has no meaning for a company or its products.

Building Brand-driven Business: Even When SMEs have the Opportunity, They Throw It Away

By 2008, the Guptas (name changed) had three manufacturing units to produce auto components. One unit was in Gurgaon (Haryana), another in Noida (UP) and the third in Jamshedpur (Jharkhand). Each unit had a different name. In early 2009, the Guptas acquired a foundry unit near Delhi to produce castings. Besides using castings for their own captive consumption, these could be sold to other auto component manufacturing units. This implied the Guptas would be marketing to their own competitors who were in the business of producing auto components. Recognizing that their competitors would become their customers, they felt that they should name their fourth unit differently. This according to the

Guptas, would prevent their customers to know that the fourth unit of castings does not belong to them. According to them, the customers may not buy from them if they learn that the Guptas—who were earlier their competitors—are also now their suppliers. When asked as to why they do not consider merging all units under one umbrella brand, the short answer was: 'We never thought of this.' The Guptas are not alone: millions of B2B marketers are in this camp. Forget about building a bigger and well-known company through building a strong brand; the idea of leveraging and unleashing potential through brand and branding does not come to their minds. I often wonder is it ignorance, indifference or sheer laziness. But it is never too late to start thinking of building business around 'brand'. It could make the difference. And like the Guptas, they are also living in their 'make believe' world that a different name would prevent their anonymity with their customers.

Brands Rejuvenate and Create Excitement

Aiming to become a strong brand has the power to rejuvenate the entire organization. When Tata Steel decided to sell its cold roll sheets as 'Steelium', it helped Tata Steel to energize and excite its own plant people. Every individual in the new cold rolling plant is aware of the difference between the cold rolled coils produced for 'Steelium' and those produced for trade, i.e., sold through channel members. Steelium is a superior product for the automotive segment. This keeps everyone in the mill to remain on toes and avoid any slips before shipping the steel to very demanding customers like Maruti, Toyota, Hyundai and Tata Motors.

Perceptions are Sticky

ABC has been in the field of bulk material handling for over 40 years. Natrajan (name changed) became the MD in late 2007. Being part of a very well-respected business house, it enjoys the image of being a trustworthy and reliable company. Though not belonging to cutting edge technology, ABC's products are considered good value for money. Its business is divided into two groups. One is around standard products used in the material handling systems which include idlers, rollers, screen vibrators, crushers, and so on. The other is project group. In its history of 40 years, a major issue with ABC has been the timely execution of the projects. The reasons could be several. One set could be due to customers. The other set could be related to internal issues—delayed purchasing of the bought outs; lack of facilities in time at the customer site; and so on. Barely within few months of becoming the MD, Natrajan was shocked to learn that even after the technical approval and lowest price, a client refused to place order on ABC. Hearing this, Natrajan rushed to Mumbai to meet the client. He was more upset about losing the order from a client who had never done business with ABC. Natrajan's assesment was that this client could not have had any view or perception about his company. But the opening remark of the client completely bowled Natrajan: 'Tell me, has ABC completed any project in time?' Obviously, the news of ABC's poor and delayed execution had reached this client too. Having heard such strong comments, Natrajan did not feel like making any sales pitch. He was willing to lose the order. But after returning to ABC's headquarter, his fist concern was to change the perception. This was to improve the project execution processes and cap-abilities of ABC. Natrajan was aware that only excellence and timely execution can alone change the experiences and perception his clients had of his company.

The Emotional Connect of Brand

I share a story of one Mr Mathur in seminars on customer satisfaction and care. He was the GM, Materials, of a well-known multinational corporation (MNC) in the field of electronic entertainment. Mr Mathur's company used to import resistors and capacitors from a small supplier in Japan. These are very small electronic components used to make printed circuit boards (PCBs). These PCBs are then used to manufacture TV and radio sets. Once Mr Mathur got an opportunity to visit Japan. As this was to be his first trip, he was keen to visit some manufacturing units of Japan. He felt that perhaps he would receive a VIP-like response if he visited the supplier against whom his company had complaints. For this, he requested his team to identify such a supplier. Despite searching several files, the team found none. The absence of complaints brought Mr Mathur discontentment. Looking at his disappointment, a team member, after great hesitation, shared that there was one supplier from Japan they had complaint against: they found, at times, that the wires which form the two ends of these resistors and capacitors moved a bit. These wires, for the purpose of packaging, are pasted on a paper board. On one paper board, some 10–15 resistors are pasted. A bundle of five of 10 paper boards is then put in small boxes for dispatch. The team member informed though there has never been any problem regarding the quality of resistors, at times they found that for some, and these could be one-in-a-million kind of a situation, the wire moved, i.e., instead of remaining straight, the resistor mounted on the board thereby looking a little out of line. He then wondered whether this could ever be seen as a complaint. He summed up by saying that an issue of this trivial nature could not and should not be considered a complaint or problem.

As Mr Mathur had no complaint from any of the other Japenese manufacturer, he thought of using this lone experience to visit a supplier in Japan. So he wrote a letter mentioning the nature of the complaint and also his plan to visit Japan. Prompt came the response requesting Mr Mathur to visit the factory. Mr Mathur now was a happy man as he could now line up at least one visit to the factory of a Japanese manufacturer!

As programmed, he visited the factory. The moment he entered the premises of the small factory, Mr Mathur was escorted to a conference room where he found eight executives around the table with samples of resistors they manufactured pasted on the paper board. All the eight executives were representing various departments like design, production, dispatch, inspection, and so on, each with the intent of trying to find out how his department could have contributed to the problem of 'moved wires'. Looking at this, Mr Mathur felt nervous. He could not believe there would be such a serious investigation for such a 'trivial' issue. He wanted the meeting to be over as soon as possible. As he went on with it, he had nothing to share beyond what he had mentioned in his letter.

Mr Mathur felt relieved after the meeting got over. But the second episode, as he was leaving the factory, came to his surprise. At the gate he found the same eight executives standing in a line with their hands folded and heads bowed. This was to express, that they were sorry for the inconvenience caused to him. This gesture, as confessed by him, brought tears in Mr Mathur's eyes.

For an insipid ingredient like resistors, which are produced and used in billions, a marketer may not even dream of developing a campaign like 'Intel Inside'. But then they would get several opportunities to create an emotional connect. And this connect is what converts a product into a brand.

When It Comes to Performance, Everything Matters

After substantial effort and time, the second largest refractory manufacturer of India could get a trial order from Nippon Steel of Japan. At one point of time, Nippon Steel was the largest steel producer around the globe. It had the reputation of being a very demanding customer competing against well-known and established European manufacturers. For an Indian refractory manufacturer a trial order from Nippon was a big breakthrough-cum-achievement. Refractories are ceramic products which can withstand very high temperatures. Steel cannot be produced without refracatories. Refractories are used in two forms, shaped like bricks and blocks and castables like cement. The bricks for trial order were dispatched with a lot of care. After a month, the supplier received a letter of appreciation from Nippon Steel, accompanied by an album containing several photographs. The letter stated that the bricks performed much better than the competing brands. However, Nippon's letter requested the supplier to improve product presentation. This suggestion was essentially to improve packaging. The photographs in the album showed packaging of bricks in different forms. Thus:

- One set of photographs shared the disappearance of all identification marks.
- The second set showed opening of the sidewalls of the wooden boxes. Several nails could be seen reflective of the fact that nails used were not of desired quality.
- The third set showed the bricks inside the box. When these were unwrapped, it was found that some of the bricks had slanted. This indicated that the bricks, due to poor packaging, must have moved during shipping.
- The fourth set of photographs showed bricks with broken or chipped edges. Though with the help of little cement these bricks could be restructured and used, Nippon Steel was looking for perfection in every aspect.

The message of the story is simple and powerful: No matter what the nature of the product may be—a product like refractory is a consumable whose identity can never be known to any steel consumer—every aspect of customer's experience creates and affects the brand.

If Brands are so Important, Why Do B2B Marketers Not Think of Creating Strong Brands?

A senior marketing executive of Tata Steel shared that many B2B marketers seem to confuse branding with 'packaging' and low advertising expenses. They feel that absence of these imply no scope for branding for B2B markets. To majority, B2B brand as an idea is very hazy. The executive identified several reasons due to which B2B marketers fail to create brands. Some of these are as follows:

- They do not have clarity on what exactly are customer needs and benefits. It requires rigorous processes to identify these. Spending money for such consumer research is beyond the means of many B2B marketers.

- They do not use channels (distributors and retailers) to reach their customers. This implies a more narrow customer base requiring no communication and selling efforts beyond personal selling.
- Majority of B2B marketers still suffer from 'volume' mentality. With this kind of mindset, the idea of brand would never even germinate.

According to the same executive, one cannot build a strong brand unless he is clear of customer advantages which the brand can deliver and then create competitive advantage for the marketers.

The Ultimate Payoff: Brand Forces You to Think

In the late 1990s, I had a chance to conduct several workshops to strengthen the competitiveness of milk cooperatives of several states. This was the initiative of National Dairy Development Board (NDDB). Prior to conducting these workshops, I also interacted with several MDs of dairies located in different cities of India. Amongst them was one Mr Dholakia of Baroda Dairy. Baroda Dairy is part of Gujarat Cooperative Milk Marketing Federation (GCMMF), which owns one of the most famous brand of India—Amul—for milk and milk products. Prior to joining GCMMF, Baroda Dairy was marketing its own brands in the local markets of Baroda. When asked about his experience of marketing under Amul, Mr Dholakia's immediate reaction was that it has taken away all the challenges and excitement. He continued that marketing of their brands was giving opportunities to create their own competencies and capabilities. With the disappearance of these opportunities, they are now a mere production unit trying to maintain quality and delivery compliance.

As a reflection, Mr Dholakia's remarks fits well with the deprivation that a large number of B2B marketers have created for themselves by not thinking of building brands. Left to itself, Baroda Dairy and its brands were almost insignificant in front of a brand like Amul. But, small or big, as reflected through the quantum of marketing and promotional spend, branding and its management requires 'thinking'. Yes, brands force the marketers to think. This, to my mind, is their biggest contribution to any organization.

Summing Up

The anecdotes and views shared in this chapter bring home a simple point that each and every action and decision affects brand. Brands in this sense become what Scott Bedbury (2002: xiii) has observed: 'Brand building is a process that when it works well should leave no facet of a company untouched. And no business practice unexamined.'

2

We are no doubt in the Great Age of the Brand.

—Tom Peter

~~~   ~~~

What is a brand? A singular idea or concept that you own inside the mind of the prospect.

—Al Ries

2

Organizational Buying and Role of Brands: The Indian Perspective

Brand and branding decisions are rooted in the context of several factors. Some of these are product-market characteristics, nature of buying and buying behaviour of the organizational customers and competitive environment. Excellent suggestions are available from the authors in the areas of marketing management such as Kotler and Keller (2006), Alexander et al. (1967), Webster (1984), Ames and Hlavacek (1984), Hutt and Speh (2007) and Anderson and Narus (2003). Readers would also benefit by reading books by Porter (1980), Prahalad and Hamel (1994) and many more in the area of strategic management to get a feel of understanding and shaping competitive strategies. Similarly, books on Brand Management by Keller (2008), Aaker and Joachimsthaler (2000), Aaker (1996), Kotler and Pfoertsch (2006) and Hague and Jackson (1994) would provide deeper insights in the area of Brand Management. My purpose is not to repeat what has been written elsewhere. My concern in this chapter is to provide an Indian perspective of the B2B markets of some well-known concepts and characteristics. With the help of the discussion in this chapter, the reader should be able to grasp well the following debate: Whether to brand or not to brand. It would also help in understanding the challenges of branding for B2B brands.

Part I

Many facets of business markets

The invisible hand of business marketing

It is widely known that nearly 50–60 per cent of the gross domestic product (GDP) of any country is being managed through the exchanges within the domain of business marketing (B2B). Thus, considering India's GDP as US$ 1,200 billion in 2008, nearly US$ 700 billion of the economy would be managed by activities and exchanges belonging to the discipline of industrial or B2B marketing. It is like the invisible hand driving the wheel of economy. Box 2.1 shares the evolution of the discipline of B2B marketing. Small or big, all organizations depend and benefit from the transactions of B2B marketing.

Box 2.1   The Graduation of Industrial Marketing to Business Marketing

Till the late 1960s, the most commonly used term was industrial marketing. This had a connotation of dealing with firms which were essentially producing industrial products. The word industrial gave a feeling that the scope covered only manufacturing firms as customers of the industrial market. Soon several authors realized the narrowness of the scope of the word 'industrial marketing'. So by the 1970s, authors started using the word 'organizational marketing' or marketing to organizational customers. This widened the scope. It appeared an all-inclusive term used to cover all types of organizations: manufacturing; institutional and government. The late 1980s saw the emergence of the term 'business-to-business marketing'. The increasing popularity of information technology (IT) in mid-1990s made popular terms like B2B, B2C, B2G, C2C, and so on.

By 2000, the term 'business marketing' seemed to have become the most commonly used term for what began as industrial marketing. Business Marketing, to majority of readers, may appear, as if the discipline covers only profit and commercial organizations. But in essence, it covers all 'for profit' and 'not for profit' organizations. To me, the most appropriate term for this discipline should be 'Organizational Marketing'. But keeping the current popular usage, this book too would be using the term Business Marketing or B2B marketing.

Consider a company like Hindustan Unilever Limited (HUL). Most of its products are sold as brands to household customers. These are classified as fast moving consumer goods (FMCG). In order to produce products like shampoos, facial creams, detergents, bathing soaps, tooth paste and other similar products, it needs to procure a variety of raw materials, plastic and paper containers, fragrances, oils and other maintenance and replacement items. Marketing of all these products would be performed by companies and individuals classified as B2B marketers. Each, in its own right, would classify as the B2B brand for HUL. Further, in order to produce the end products HUL requires process plants, packaging plants, conveyer equipments and several other capital goods. For its research and development (R&D) labs, it would need many sophisticated testing equipments. For all these, it would require a big procurement department. But this huge purchasing activity would never be seen or known to its end-user/customers. The housewife who uses such products would never be able to even figure out as to who supplied millions of plastic bottles or billions of laminated sachets to pack the shampoo she uses. But the truth is, all that she uses has been made possible with the efforts of business marketing and B2B brands.

What is true for FMCG brands of HUL would also be true for the endless list of products for household markets like shirts, saris, cars, television (TV) sets, refrigerators, household appliances, etc.

The domain of business marketing

Before a product or even service reaches its end-user/customer, it passes through several exchanges of value additions. These value additions are provided by different constituents of the value chain of the whole economy. This value chain would vary for each product category or of an industry. Conceptually, it would appear similar for all the goods sold in the economy. Figure 2.1 provides a conceptual view of this value chain and the stages for each type of industry in the economy. As evident from the figure, the first five stages of the value chain belong to the domain of B2B marketing. All the exchanges and transactions are managed by the efforts of B2B marketers. It is only the last stage which truly belongs to the

Figure 2.1 The Value Chain of an Economy

First Raw Material Extraction	*Second* Material Processing	*Third* Manufacturing	*Fourth* Final Assembly	*Fifth* Distribution and After Markets	*Sixth* Wholesales and Retail Sales to Household Consumers
					Domain of B2C Brands
		Domain of B2B Brands: Organizations in the chain			
First ONGC Oil India Reliance Industries Coal India Tata Steel	*Second* Indian Oil Tata Steel Reliance Industries Sterlite Hindalco	*Third* L&T Bharat Forge Sundaram Fasteners Sona Steering Rane Brakeline	*Fourth* Tata Motors Maruti Godrej Boyce LG Nokia, HUL	*Fifth* Dealers Service Providers	

Source: Ames and Hlavacek (1984: 19).

consumer or B2C marketing. But being the last and the most visible phase of marketing activity, it tends to give an impression as if marketing as a discipline only belongs to B2C brands.

The domain of B2B, as seen from Figure 2.1, could contain thousands of products to produce B2C brands. Thus, a male shirt needs approximate 12 items to be stiched, from thread to cotton, while a car needs around 10,000 components to be built. So a generalized treatment, though unavoidable, would always fail to capture the specificity of the branding challenges for thousands of B2B brands. Each marketer before initiating the branding decisions would benefit by mapping the product market and competition context relevant for his organization.

The scope and range of B2B products

If one examines the buying basket of a typical manufacturing organization like BHEL, HMT, HUL, Tata Motors, Reliance Industries, Arvind Mills or L&T, one would soon discover that all these organizations bought some plants and machinery at some point of time. Each year they may buy some induction motors, electrical switchgears, transformers, valves and pumps. They may also buy computers, telephone equipment, inspection and quality control equipments. These organizations also buy, on a regular basis, raw material. Thus, Reliance Refinery would need crude oil; L&T would need cement and steel; Arvind Mills would need cotton, dyes and chemicals, and pigments; Tata Motors would purchase steel, plastic and other form of raw material to produce cars and trucks. The same organizations also purchase oil for fuel, lubrications, paper for photocopying, bulbs and tube lights for offices and packaging material for the final packing of goods they produce. The list would soon run into thousands or may be millions of items. The scope is very vast. But this variety can be conceptualized in several ways as seen from the following discussion.

B2B product classification

Authors have conceptualized the organizational basket in several ways. Amongst some popularly used classifications, one was by Vitale and Giglierano (2002: 37, 38).

- Material and parts, e.g., raw materials, manufactured materials and parts.
- Capital items, e.g., buildings, equipments used in buyer's production, operations.
- Supplies and services, e.g., operating supplies, repair and maintenance item.

Another classification was suggested by Alexander et al. (1967: 22). Their classification was:

- Major capital equipments
- Minor capital equipments
- Components
- Consumables
- Processed material and chemicals
- Office equipments
- Services

These can further be classified in two broad categories: 'capital goods' and 'revenue purchases.'

The capital goods

These become part of the balance sheet and are shown as fixed assets.

1. **Major capital equipments:** These are needed to produce the end products. The buying of major capital equipments is not very frequent. These involve commitment of long-term capital by the organizations. Selection of technology and negotiations for the commercial terms become very critical. Buying of capital equipments would imply high involvement of a large group. Each capital project would need several types of capital equipments. Thus, a steel plant would need blast furnace, steel-making furnaces, oxygen plants, compressors, power generating sets, sintering plants, heating furnaces and continuous casting machines. The buying criteria would include several parameters of performance. For the marketers

the customer base would be very narrow. Both buying and selling would be very specialized tasks. Being very critical to the success of business, strong brands would be preferred.

2. **Minor capital equipments**: These include products like electrical motors and pumps, valves, greasing and maintenance equipments, welding machines, grinders, desktop computers, printers, copiers, and so on. These may be more like standard products and not tailor-made for the customers. They have low purchase value. But these are still part of the fixed assets of the organization. Depending on the nature of the products, the customer could be narrow or broad. Strong brands would be preferred for most of the products.

The revenue items

These items are listed under the profit and loss statements on the balance sheet of an organization. These account for a large portion of the annual purchasing done by organizations like HUL, Maruti, Mahindra and Mahindra, SAIL, and thousands of large, medium, small and tiny sector organizations. The buying effort is enormous for organizations like Maruti, Ashok Leyland, LG and Hyundai Motors. These organizations would classify as original equipment manufactures (OEM). They depend very substantially on bought-outs, i.e., outsourcing from a select group of vendors. Selection and development of vendors require enormous organizational efforts and energy. As the quality of vendors can provide sustainable competitiveness, the management of these is very strategic. These include:

1. **Raw materials**: A major component of the cost of goods sold is raw material. These may account for as high as 60–70 per cent of the cost in the case of processed industries like aluminum, petroleum refineries, copper and zinc, sulphuric acid, steel, and so on. Similar to these, the other manufacturing units too would need raw material to produce the end product. Thus, Godrej Boyce would need cold rolled sheets and coils to produce their office furniture like filing cabinets, almirhas or steel furniture; Advani Oerilkon would

need electrode grade wire rods to produce welding electrodes; Usha Martin would need special grade wire rods to make wires and finally the wire ropes. Being critical in terms of commercial value and risk, top management would always get involved in the buying of raw materials. Even though majority may appear as commodities due to stiff competition, marketers are trying to create brands to move buyers away from the price issues.

2. **Components:** These are needed to make end products like TVs, cell phones, refrigerators, washing machines, bicycles, scooters, cars and a whole host of end products. These items could be tailor-made or be proprietary items of the marketers (electrical starters, bearings, electrical motors, horns, pumps, tubes and TV tubes are some handy examples). These components do not lose their identity. The most common and highly visible example of a component is the famous 'Intel chip' for personal computers (PCs). 'Intel Inside' is a classic case of a component hidden inside, but due to a very creative punch-line it has created tremendous visibility. The success of Intel has become a major motivator for B2B brands.

3. **Consumables:** Consumables are needed to run plants and machinery. Thus, lubricating oil, grease and refractories are needed to run the plants. Paper is needed to get the printouts; grinding wheels and electrodes are needed to produce the end products; conveyer belts are needed to transfer material from one place to other; idlers and rollers are needed to run the conveyor belts and pulleys are needed to run the same belt; scrappers are needed to clean the belts; guides are needed to ensure that the material does not fall off the belts. For a manufacturing or a process plant, the list would be long. As the name suggests, the life is limited for consumables. Due to this, buying is very regular for some fast moving, i.e., frequently used consumables. Some of these would be like toners for a copier, paper for the printers and plain paper copier, lubricating oil for the machine tools and welding electrodes. For some, the frequency of replacement may be less. Some examples are electrical items like cables, lugs for cable terminations or electrical contactors for motor starters.

Some authors call these as MROs or maintenance, repairs and operating equipments. For majority of these items, well-known brands would be preferred. But for several of these purchasers, especially government organizations, the preference would be on the lowest price basis. Strong brands with premium may lose out in such situations.

But even then, as these offer a major scope for cost reductions, organizations in India have become very careful in examining the usage patterns and life of these consumables. The earlier criterion of buying these at the lowest price for the approved suppliers is giving way to superior products, i.e., known brands from more credible suppliers.

4. **Processed materials and chemicals**: Even though these are consumables, they need to be classified separately because the difference lies is in their end use. These are used as ingredients in producing a product and lose their identity once used. A handy example could be the salt, spices and edible oil in producing potato chips. Similarly while producing castings, many foundries would use chemicals and additives to make moulds and alloys for the steel or iron which is being used to produce the castings. Another example could be the use of chemicals and additives to produce ready mix concrete. The quality of these materials is very critical to ensure the performance or quality of the end product. Thousands of colours, pigments and chemicals are used to produce coloured and printed fabric for garments. A minor variation in the quality of these can play havoc with the quality of the end product. Though these may account for a very low percentage of the total coast in the fabric and final garment, if the colour fades or smudges, the damage to the brand of the product—shirt or sari—would be enormous. Hence, the buyers do not take risks and prefer to deal with tested and reliable brands.

5. **Services**: Besides the tangible products, B2B customers need several services. One end of this spectrum could be financial services. The other end could be the canteen and catering

services. In between could lie several other services like head hunters, contractors of labour, civil works, security, transporters, gardeners, and so on. Infosys, Accenture, FedEx, UPS, BM, all are very big and widely known service brands. On the other hand, there are thousands of local suppliers who also need to appear as good brands to their customers.

6. **Office equipments:** A separate mention of office eqipments is to highlight the importance of these assets and purchases of an organization. Furniture, air conditioning equipments, computers, plain paper copiers, audio visual aids like projectors, etc., would come under this category. For an educational institution like XLRI these would classify as major capital items. Similar would be the case for other institutions like banks and large number of service-oriented government and non-government organizations (NGOs). In many organizations these are purchased on the basis of annual rate contracts. Brands do play a very important role. Some 10–15 years back, local brands in air conditioners, computers or office furniture had become a major threat to the well-known brands. But post 2000, due to reforms in the tax structure, the well-known brands have regained the lost markets.

The B2B customer: Some unique dimensions

B2B marketing deals with organizational customers

Though a very simple point, one must always remember that B2B marketing deals with situations where customers are organizations. These may belong to manufacturing organizations or service organizations. These may be owned by the government like central or state and public sector organizations. These could be large, medium or small organizations.

Table 2.1 provides an approximate number of organizations in India. It indicates that India had around 17.5 million organizations which could be considered as B2B customers. If we include even 10 per cent of the retail outlets then the number could be around 20 million.

Table 2.1 Organizational Customers in India, 2008

Category	Total No.
Primary and elementary schools [a, c]	2,497,585
Upper primary schools [a, c]	1,229,652
High schools [a, c]	106,024
Colleges [a]	20,760
Universities [a]	382
Professional institutions [a]	7,120
Government organizations [b]	1,222
NGOs [b]	180
Number of registered companies [a]	855,516
Number of registered SMEs [a]	2,031,910
Number of un-registered SMEs [a]	10,811,864
PSUs [b]	1,669
Total	17,563,884 (17.5 million)
Retail outlets [d]	12 million in total
	5 million for food and related products
Grand total	29.5 million

Sources: [a] Indiastat, [b] GOI website, [c] DISE edu stats, [d] India retail show.

Buying is on behalf and purposive

No matter who buys in the organization, the CEO or a lower level clerk, the buying in an organization is always on its behalf. This 'buying on behalf' restricts freedom, creates more accountability and demands transparency of the decision makers and B2B customers. As buying is on behalf of the organizations, it may be safe to state that most of the purchases in an organizations would be for a purpose. Depending upon the nature of the product, the purpose would also differ. Thus, components like tyres, steering wheels, horns and brake linings are needed to make a truck or car. The quantity of items needed would be linked to the productions plans of the truck manufacturers. The purchasers would not be able to buy more even if these products are sold at half the price. The buyer would be constrained by several economic and non-economic considerations. For example, if it is buying a plant, it would be for producing the products; if it is furniture, it would be for the offices of the employees; if it is an air conditioner, it would be to provide a comfortable atmosphere to be more productive. One can argue that this could be true for a large number of purchases by household customers also. But unlike the organizational customer, who would have to justify the need both in terms of quantity and problem or objective being achieved, household customers do not have to justify him or her purchase to any one. He or she is accountable only to himself or herself. Thus, where the buying is purposive for organizational customers, the same by the individual could be a combination of purpose and impulse. In such a scenario, buyers may not be able to justify buying of brands at higher prices. But as shared in Chapter 1, organizational customers, irrespective of their size and ownership, would still prefer well-known brands.

The techno commercial need of the buyer must be met

No matter what they buy, vegetables, cooking oil, a very sophisticated machine tool, a software package like enterprise resource planning (ERP) or a power generating equipment, all buying is finally based on some specifications of quality, performance parameters and physical dimensions like size, shape, weight or chemical properties. Besides these, the buyers would also specify its delivery expectations, payment terms and other commercial terms. The buyers would expect its suppliers to meet both the technical specifications and commercial terms and conditions. Even when suppliers may try to modify these to their advantage, in the end, the marketer would have to satisfy technical and commercial conditions of the buyers. Could brand be a substitute? The answer is both 'Yes' and 'No'. It depends on the nature of the product and the preference of the buyers for branded products.

Narrow customer base

For most of the B2B products, market base, i.e., the number of customers, is limited. This number may vary from product to product, but as compared to household markets, where the number would run into millions, the number for majority of B2B products and services may not exceed thousands. However, for products like computers, ceiling fans, stationery items and certain category of appliances, it would be a hybrid market, implying a very large customer base. The narrow customer base enables easy identification of customers. Direct distribution and personal selling would be the dominant vehicle for communication and selling. Relationship with the buyers would also play a critical role in determining business success.

If the base is not narrow, the marketers with large customer base would have to perform the marketing task similar to B2C marketing. The broad customer base would require indirect distribution, i.e., use intermediaries, create brands and rely on several communication mix elements besides personal selling.

For most of the B2B marketers low product visibility, narrow customer base, predominance of personal selling and importance of relationship are the commonly cited reasons for low concern for branding.

The derived demand situation

The term 'derived demand' means that the demand of industrial products and services is a function of the demand of the end products where they are used. Thus, demand of tyres will depend upon the demand of cars, trucks, tractors and two wheelers like scooters and motor cycles. Moving a step backward on the value chain, the demand of natural rubber would depend on the demand of several end uses where rubber is used. This would include tyres of all types, tubes and conveyer belts, rubber liners for material handling equipment, several household products, toys, and so on. Similarly a manufacture producing cold rolled thin steel sheets would realize that the demand of its steel sheets would be dependent on the demand of products like cars, home appliances like TV sets, refrigerators, air conditioners, ceiling fans, personal computers, steel cabinets, and so on. For a product like tin plate the demand would depend upon the demand for the metal containers for food items, paints, milk powder, bottle enclosures, battery jackets, and so on. For a utility product like electricity, demand would be dependent upon the demand of the industries, service organizations and household segment. The demand for steel would generate demand for steel plants and its equipments. Demand for cars would create demand for several forms of capital equipments like presses to transform the sheets, paint shops, assembly plants, several machine tools and grinding machines. With this characteristic of demand, many B2B marketers feel that the demand for their product and service is fixed and no amount of brand-building

Chicago State University

effort would help them to increase the demand for their products. This is a misplaced notion. A strong brand is needed for superior performance, price premium and market share.

The greater buyer–seller interdependence

For a large number of product services, there are opportunities and situations where both the buyer and seller work mutually. Manufacturers of automobiles have followed this policy for decades. The industry experts observe that nearly 75–80 per cent of a car or truck is bought out. A truck has more than 8,000–10,000 components made from different material like steel, rubber, plastic, nylon or aluminum. These are forgings, castings, gears, dash boards, bulbs, light covers, brake lining, fuel injection pumps, steering wheels, seats, and so on. From mere vendors to strategic partnership are the policies which buyers and sellers follow. In this kind of a situation, performance is reflected through quality of product, and service is reflected through responsiveness and reliability and relationship management. Finally, the source credibility gets rewarded. The same interdependence would be true for thousands of other products belonging to different industries covering various stages of the value chain.

The organizational buying situations and role of brands

All organization buying can be classified around three buying situations or tasks (Kotler and Pfoertsch 2006: 25). These are: straight re-buy or re-buy situations; modified re-buy situations; and new-buy or new-task situations (Kotler and Pfoertsch 2006: 50). Kotler and Pfoertsch feel that strong brands may be more effective for the new-buy situations in contrast to the repeat buy situations. But my personal view is that brands would be effective in all the mentioned situations. This gets reflected when organizations demonstrate brand loyalty in repeat or straight re-buy situations.

Organizational buying behaviour (OBB): Some unique characteristics

There are four buying behaviour characteristics which are unique to a majority of B2B buyers. Leaving aside the exceptions, it is my view that these would cut across for most of the B2B customers.

1. **Buying is procedural**: No matter how small or big the organization is, each organization follows the laid-down processes and policies. As is known, buying would start by developing and issuing a 'request for purchase' (RFP). Large organizations belonging to the government would advertise in newspapers. Small organizations may pick up a phone or send an e-mail to seek proposal. Following the process is a must for both the buyers and marketers. There should not be any shortcuts. But as mentioned a strong brand can shorten the entire process, reduce the total buying effort and lead to a win-win situation for both.

2. **Buying is multiperson**: It is widely known that the buying process and the final act of buying decision involve many persons. This multi-person involvement has been conceptualized as the concept of 'buying centre' or BC (Webster and Wind 1972: 33–37). The concept means that during the entire process of buying, the various members appear to play different roles. The original concept had identified five different roles: influencers; deciders; users; buyers and gatekeepers. Subsequently roles like specifires, indenters and initiators have also been added. The idea of BC is broader than the idea of decision making units (DMUs). DMU covers only the 'deciders'. The B2B marketers have to influence not only the members of DMU, but also the members of BC. There are several studies which show that many B2B marketers find it difficult to know all the members of the BC and their role in buying decision. Strong brands become a big asset to influence the members of the BCs even when they are not known to the sales persons of the B2B marketers.

3. **Lag between marketing effort and results**: Due to procedures and multi-person involvement, B2B marketers would always find a considerable time lag between their efforts and the final results. This leads to the conclusion that organizational buying cannot be impulsive or instinctive. Based on this one may argue for a lesser role and power of strong brands. But as we would soon observe in the fourth characteristics of OBB, this delay in buying may not come against strong brands.

4. **The ultimate buying decisions are both rational and emotional:** The observation made earlier was that buying process and multi-person involvement may make buying appear more rational. But the experience of millions of buying situations reveals that it is a myth that all B2B buying decisions are rational and devoid of emotionality. This is because even in organizations, only human beings are involved in buying decisions. This, to my mind, is a very strong case for having an emotional connect via brands. Kotler and Pfoertsch (2006: 58) too have supported this view.

Part II

Are brands relevant for B2B marketers: What empirical studies reveal

The presence of hyper competition, increasing buying complexities in limited time with abundant information overload and globalization and pressures on prices are the developments which would make brands more and more relevant for the B2B customers. Kotler and Pfoertsch (2006: 46) have quoted an MCM–McKinsey study. This study collected information from 750 deciders to determine the important function of brands in B2B marketing. Though conducted in Germany, the authors feel that the findings would be relevant globally. The German study identified three important functions. These were: information efficiency, risk reduction and value/image creation. Out of these, risk reduction (45 per cent) is the most important function in the B2B area. This is followed by information efficiency (41 per cent) and the least important was image creation (14 per cent).

Kotler and Pfoertsch (2006: 52) further suggested that brands help marketers to differentiate, build brand loyalty, create preferences, command premium, differentiate marketing efforts and finally, increase the sales.

The Indian scenario

Almost similar to the MCM–McKinsey study on the role and importance of B2B brands, we at XLRI (a leading post-graduate business school of India) have been conducting several studies to understand the role and relevance of brands for B2B customers. Spread over a period of nearly 10 years, these studies examined questions like:

- What attributes do the B2B customers consider for their buying decisions?
- What importance do they give to various attributes in buying different products?
- Does the importance of attributes and brands vary across different product categories?
- Do brands have different roles in different buying situations?
- Does the preference amongst the various members of the BC vary for brands?
- Are they willing to pay premium for brands?
- Do B2B customers give importance to brands in their buying decisions?

These studies covered both multi-product and multi companies, as well as in-depth study of single companies. The salient points are shared in the remaining portion of the chapter.

Organizational buying decisions:
A multi-product–multi-company study

This study, which covered 60 respondents and four B2B organizations, revealed that, by and large, majority of the B2B buyers use a combination of nearly 12 factors in their buying decisions. Eight of these would come under tangible or rational factors. The remaining four belong to intangible and emotional factors. Figure 2.2 provides the consolidated findings. Readers would sense the prevalence of a 70:30 situation. Seventy per cent of a buying decision is influenced by tangible or rational factors and the remaining 30 per cent is accounted by the intangible factors. These intangibles are part of brand image and perceptions. Kotler and Pfoertsch (2006: 33) have classified these as hard and soft factors.

Figure 2.2   Buying Attributes and Their Importance

Tangibles/Rational Factors		Emotional/Intangibles Factors	
Attributes	Importance (%)	Attributes	Importance (%)
1. Quality	10	9. Reputation of supplier	7.36
2. Performance	9.38	10. Reliability	9.72
3. Delivery fulfilment	8.65	11. Brand	7.57
4. After sales service	8.60	12. Relationship with suppliers	6.69
5. Price	8.26		
6. Availability	8.30		
7. Ease of maintenance	7.87		
8. Ease of operation	7.52		
Total	**70%**	**Total**	**30%**

Source: Author.

Buying decisions and influence of brands in a large steel company

The second study conducted on a large steel company indicated that decision making is based on both rational (past experience, domain knowledge and price) and emotional and subjective factors reflected through experience and perception of a brand. The study showed the average importance of four factors in buying of several products by the B2B customers which is shown in Table 2.2.

Table 2.2   Factors Enabling Decision Making

Rational Factors		*Emotional Factor*	
1. Price	32%	Brand	26%
2. Domain knowledge	21%		
3. Past experience	21%		
Total	74%		

The study analysed the data for different product categories purchased by the steel company. Table 2.3 illustrates the details.

This study almost supports the 70:30 ratio of the study covering multi-product and multi-company situation discussed earlier (see Figure 2.2).

The study on the steel plant also identified the influence of members of the BC in the steel company. It indicated the influence of the various members of the BC as shown in Table 2.4. With such a strong influence of top management, strong brands would always help.

Brand effects: The case of a tube company

The third study was conducted to understand the role of brands in a tube manufacturing company. The study examined the influence of brands on members of the BC for specific products belonging to different product categories. The findings are shown in Table 2.5. As would be seen, irrespective of the product, brands have high influence on both the deciders and buyers.

Buying situations where brands have more influence

A fourth study examined the influence of brands in different buying situations. The findings are shown in Table 2.6.

Table 2.6 indicates that except where relationship with the existing supplier is more important, strong brands are perceived to be influencing buying decisions in several buying situations.

The same study indicated that 70 per cent of material personnel attach more importance in buying from the reputed suppliers. Fifty-five per cent of the material personnel indicated that they were willing to readily accept new products from suppliers of reputed brands. This indicates that a strong brand and reputation of suppliers can facilitate easy and faster acceptance of new products.

Premium for the brands

The fourth study revealed that nearly 65 per cent members of the BC are willing to pay premium for branded products. The price premium ranged from 2.5 to 80 per cent!

Table 2.3 Important Factors in Buying Decision

Product Category	Product Item	Brands Used	Price	Domain Knowledge of Supplier	Past Experience	Brand
• Raw material	Sponge iron	Tata Sponge Jindal Bihar Sponge	40%	25%	5%	30%
• Major capital items	Level 2 automation	POSCO	NA	40%	20%	40%
• Minor capital items	Laptops	IBM, HP	20%	30%	10%	40%
• Components	Bearings	SKF, Tata Bearing	10%	20%	30%	40%
• Processed materials and chemicals	Water treatment injection chemicals	Vasu Chemicals, Betz	20%	30%	30%	20%
• Process consumables	Electrode	• Orlicon • Fontec • Modiarc • Esab	25%	10%	30%	35%
• General consumables	Safety helmets	NA	60%	NA	40%	NA
• Office equipments	Stationery	NA	90%	NA	10%	NA
• Services	IT services	TTIL, PWC, TCS, IBM	30%	40%	20%	30%

Source: Author.

Table 2.4   Influence of Buying Centre Members in Decision Making

1. Top management	34%
2. Technical experts	27%
3. Users	23%
4. Purchase department	15%
5. Finance	1%

Source: Author.

Table 2.5   Brand Effect

		Brand Effect On	
Product Category	*Products*	*Deciders*	*Buyers*
● Raw material	PP rings	High	High
● Major capital	Laptop	High	High
● Minor capital	Printer	High	High
● Processed material and chemicals	Lubricants	High	High
● Consumables	Bearings	High	High
● Services	Pickling of coil	High	High
● Office equipments	Chairs	High	High

Source: Author.

Table 2.6   Brand Effect in Different Buying Situations

The Buying Situation	*Importance of Brands on '5' Point Scale*
● Is critical to the operations of the organization	3.68
● Where product is high-tech nature	3.57
● Buying is of high value items	3.27
● Strategically is important for the organization	3.09
● Our customer insist for the source	3.02
● Relationship with suppliers is more important	2.20

Source: Author.

On an average, strong or superior brands could command a price premium of 12.5 per cent. An interesting finding is the difference in the willingness to pay premium by material and non-material personnel as shown in Table 2.7.

Only 33 per cent of the non-material personnel felt that they would be willing to pay a price premium for branded products in B2B scenario. These non-material personnel were willing to pay a price premium of 13 per cent on an average for reputed brands.

Table 2.7 Price Premium for Branded Products (in Per Cent)

	Materials Personnel	Non-materials Personnel
Willing to pay	64	33
Not willing to pay	36	67

Source: Author.

Where brand may work

The study on steel company (the second study quoted earlier) enabled the conceptualization shown in Figure 2.3. The figure has two parameters—the status of the buyer in terms of his level of awareness and the perceived risk of the product's performance. The conclusions of Figure 2.3 are almost stating the obvious and are in line with the observations made earlier, i.e., brands are very important for B2B marketing.

Figure 2.3 Conceptualization on Importance of Brands

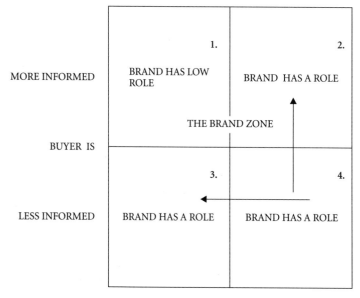

Source: Author.

Effect of brands on procurement at a large steel plant

The study on steel company also analysed the status of the brand, i.e., whether national, global and local vis-à-vis product's criticality in the quality of steel being produced. The analysis is shown in Figure 2.4. What is interesting to observe that except for Cell 3, the preference is for strong brands from the known suppliers for the other three cells. The majority of Cell 3 products would be from the local SMEs. But within these, an SME with superior image would be in an advantageous position. Even here, the brand would get preference even when it may not get the premium.

Major Conclusions of Indian Studies on Role of Brands in Organizational Buying

The Indian studies like their counterparts are echoing the same conclusions of the role of brands for B2B markets. These are:

Figure 2.4   Brand Status vis-à-vis Products' Criticality to Quality of Steel

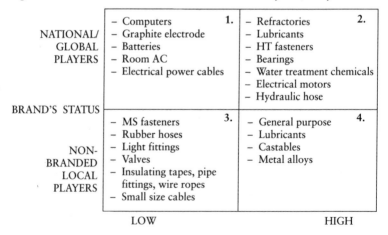

Source: Author.

- Quality is the most important ingredient for all strong brands. The claims of quality must be backed-up by performance. Minus the performance, brands would be meaningless. This conclusion is in line with what authors claim that behind every strong brand is superior product quality and service (Kotler and Keller 2006: 273).
- Strong brands would fetch premium. Studies have revealed that on a generalized basis the B2B customers may be willing to pay a price premium of 12–15 per cent for reputed brands. Exceptional situations may enable a very high premium up to 80 per cent.
- Strong brands get a larger share of the business.
- The research has shown that even for standard and routinely purchased products, the BC members develop an emotional relationship with brands. For these they are prepared to pay a price premium.
- B2B marketers have something to gain by investing in building a strong and positive brand image amongst all stakeholders.
- For many buying situations, it would be difficult to identify and influence the members of the BC. A strong brand would be an advantage, even when the marketer may fail to cover (in their selling efforts) all the members of the BCs.
- Studies reveal that a strong brand and branding are important assets for superior performance in terms of market share and profitability.
- Irrespective of the product categories, a strong brand would help in all situations—be it components, process components, major and minor capital items, and others.
- The importance and preference for brands may vary amongst the members of the BC. Users are always inclined to buy the best known brand.
- Though most of the members give maximum weightage to the rational aspects like product specifications and price, the emotional factors seem to play a role in almost all the buying situations.

- When the nature of the product is critical, the tendency of the user is to avoid any risk. Hence, they always purchase the same trusted brand, irrespective of price.
- When there are several suppliers at comparable prices, there is a tendency to buy from the supplier with a strong brand who shares a good relationship with the customers.

Summing Up

The findings and conclusion of the Indian studies seem to be in line with those made by authors like Mudambi (2002). In her article titled 'Branding Importance in Business-to-Business Markets: Three Buyer Clusters', she observes: 'A recognized brand name with positive association attached has an advantage at each stage of the decision process, even under high-learning (high-involvement) purchase situations' (Mudambi 2002: 525–33).

Nearly 40 years ago when very few authors were talking of B2B brands, Theodore Levitt, through his research on communication and industrial selling, observed that credible and strong source effect, i.e., corporate brand, has a positive role in helping the sales person to get a favourable response from industrial buyers (Levitt 1967). The findings of the Indian studies too have established, beyond any doubt, that no matter what buyers buy, they would always give preference to strong and credible B2B brands.

*In the 21st century branding will ultimately be the only
unique differential between companies.
Brand equity is now a key asset.*

—Anonymous

*If you do not have a competitive advantage,
don't compete.*

—Jack Welch

3

Brand Management and B2B Marketers: A Deeper Probe

Why Should We Brand?

It was the Brand Summit of Confederation of Indian Industries (CIIs) of the eastern region in the steel city of Jamshedpur. Besides Mr Muthuraman, ex-MD of Tata Steel, other well-known professionals of brand management of India participated in the Summit. One such participant was Mr Alyque Padmasee, ex-CEO of the then Lintas and now Lowe India. The year was 2005. Jamshedpur, besides the town of Tata Steel and Tata Motors, has several engineering and manufacturing units like Tinplate Company of India Limited (TCIL), Tata Robin Fraser (TRF), Timken, Tata Cummins, Usha Martin Industries, Tata Rolls (earlier Tata Yodogava Limited) and many more medium to large size firms. Each company is a leader in its product category. Besides these large organizations, Adityapur Industrial Development Authority would have around more than 600 small and medium size firms, majority of which would be in B2B marketing and would-be vendors to Tata Steel, Tata Motors and their associate companies. The delegates in the CII brand summit were B2B marketers. They were present to listen to the discussion on how 'brand' would be important for them. They were eager to know the concepts and experiences for creating brands for B2B markets. In his opening remarks, Mr Muthuraman shared the plans of Tata Steel to sell nearly 50 per cent of its products as branded products. Steel, for the majority, is a commodity, a raw material.

But Mr Muthuraman shared that there are nearly 20,000 varieties of steel. Each one has potential to be sold as a different brand. Through this example, he was trying to tell the audience that it is wrong and a myth to treat steel as a commodity. He also shared the examples of new brands like Tata Shakti (for galvanized steel sheets), Tata Agrico (for agricultural implements like crowbars, sickles, ploughs, *phawdas*) which Tata Steel has been marketing since 1927, Tata Steelium, the cold rolled sheets from a very sophisticated mill, Tata Structura, and few more. From the standpoint of Tata Steel, it is a wonderful achievement. Except for Steelium and Structura, the other brands are predominantly for B2C customers. These are sold through retailers or distributors. As shared by Mr Muthuraman, the experience of building brands is helping Tata Steel a great deal in not only increasing its market share but also in earning premium on its brands. Mr Alaque Padmasee was the next speaker at the Summit. The audience was looking forward to listen to the celebrity, especially flown from Mumbai. Alaque shared two audio visual presentations. First one was that of 'Liril', a bathing soap brand belonging to HUL—a soap with the freshness of lime introduced in 1975 with the help of Lintas, then headed by Alaque. Even by 2005, it was considered to be an outstanding launch. Superb positioning (exploiting the power of the freshness of lime) and an excellent execution of commercials made Liril a runaway success. As it was his creation, he had the legitimate claim for the success. Then came his second presentation. This was on Shree Cements, the TV commercial which was running on several channels in 2005. It claimed a unique benefit of preventing rusting of reinforcement bars of steel (used for reinforced concrete construction [RCC] for buildings). By virtue of the presence of red oxide as one of its ingredients, Shree Cements claimed the use of its cements would prevent rods from rusting. Thereby providing longevity to the bars—longevity being the final benefit to the buildings.

This presentation was followed by four more presentations. To the audience's disappointment none touched or shared any experience which covers the area of branding in the context of SMEs, serving markets with narrow customer base and manufacturing components and intermediaries for large customers like Tata Motors, Tata Steel, and so on. They were looking for answers to questions like: why should we worry about creating brands? What we would gain by spending money on brand-building activities? Obviously the wisdom of many could not convince the audience of Jamshedpur, predominantly a city of B2B marketers, to think of developing brand-driven business.

Since then Jamshedpur has had three such brand summits organized by CII and other professional bodies. But till June 2009, the entrepreneurs were not convinced about the payoffs from building brands or from following the concepts and numerous frameworks of brand management.

They argue that the payoffs do not justify the efforts in money and time spent in executive decisions. Executive involvement in branding decisions appear as distraction and disruptions to a large majority of B2B marketers. To them, 'brands' are the preoccupation of the marketers of products like soap and Coke. In short, brand and branding appear to be redundant.

Their views seem to get support from observations of gurus like Geoffrey Moore (2009) who feels:

> … while [branding] has extraordinary relevance to B2C volume oper-ations enterprises, it has virtually no relevance to B2B complex systems enterprises …. IBM, GE, Cisco, Oracle, SAP Siemens, Accenture and Caterpillar are great companies but it is highly misleading to think of them as great brands …. In a complex systems enterprise the mechanisms are completely different.

Though Moore's views reflect an extreme stand, the majority of B2B marketers' views on brands seem to be ambivalent and swing like a pendulum from time to time. This lack of clarity and conviction prevents B2B marketers to build brands on a sustained basis. So whatever little they do, ultimately turns out to be a slipshod and ad hoc. It is neither here nor there. Armed with this background, I tried to gain some deeper insights by interacting with senior managers representing a cross-section of products. These are being shared in the form of small caselets as follows. These would provide both a wider perspective and deeper insights.[1]

B2B brands are more than a seductive communication

Till April 2009, C.D. Kamath (CDK) was the MD of Tata Refractories Limited (TRL) for over 12 years. TRL has been the number one player all throughout its existence of 50 years in India. By 2008, its sale had crossed Rs 7,500 million (US$ 156 million).[2] It is a subsidiary of Tata Steel, the oldest and largest steel plant in the private sector of India. A simple question as to what he considers to be the role of brands for TRL provoked several remarks from CDK:

> The example of companies like Intel and IBM are not relevant for a product like refractories. Unlike Intel, which ultimately gets the benefit of B2C situations, refractory remains essentially a product for B2B markets. The buying of refractories is done by the professionals on the basis of product features. The buying decisions are influenced by the delivery of promised performance and not how marketers have packaged their products into brands. For our customers, technical and scientific information is more critical. At the end, trust in the suppliers like TRL is very important.

Continuing, CDK shared that:

> … the brand image of Tatas does play a role. The approving people, i.e., those who are placing the orders, feel reassured and comfortable while dealing with a company associated with the house of Tata: the most trusted brand of corporate India. In this sense corporate communications do play a role in creating the corporate image.

Further, CDK observed:

> TRL could never convince itself to spend money on advertising. I personally feel that spending money on mass media advertisement is a waste. We have never been clear on the returns on money spent on communications. We could not prove whether the money spent on communications would lead to higher sale or profit or both. It is for this reason that we do not indulge in any brand building activities.
>
> Nearly 75 per cent to 80 per cent of our sales are to Steel Industries. Refractories are very critical consumables for steel. Without these, steel plants would not be able to produce steel. Being so critical, steel plants employ professionals for buying refractories and even the users of refractories are very knowledgeable. Steel plants could never be influenced through seductive communications of a brand. At best, the role of communication

could be linked to creation of awareness but nothing beyond it. But for non steel customers both within India and abroad, with limited expertise and knowledge for a product like refractories, brand awareness and image will be very helpful. For global steel customers we do not need to create brand as they are very knowledgeable.

TRL's customer base would be around 100. Out of these, five large steel plants would account for 60 per cent of its sales. The other 20 mid-size steel plants would account for another 20 per cent of its sales. The remaining customers would be non-steel customers like cement, glass and petroleum. Even for these the remaining 20 customers, branding may not achieve any additional advantage. According to CDK, his knowledgeable and rational customers cannot be fooled on the basis of the 'packaging' which a consumer product company does to its products. This may be helpful for consumer products situations, but in the case of B2B situations, brands can never be created through promotions alone. It is only consistency in performance that creates the brand. Quality consistency coupled with delivery compliance and efficient service support is what creates the brand. The B2B marketers are fully aware of these facts and their role in creating strong brand.

For B2B brands, customer value and relationship management are important

When asked to share some experiences of managing brands for B2B markets, a VP of Tata Steel felt that it has done a lot in B2C, but nothing much in B2B. Reflecting a little more, he shared that for B2B markets, Tata Steel has concentrated more on customer value management (CVM), relationship management or managing the interface between customers and Tata Steel, and contract management. These initiatives have led Tata Steel to gain 45 per cent market share in flat products in India. 'This definitely is huge market share to defend especially in light of intense competition from local and global players like Nippon Steel, Posco and others', observes the VP. He recognized that association with the house of Tatas does play a very important role in conveying trust and assurance of an honest play. The Tata logo in the visiting card does matter and creates a positive image and also can get a preference from the buyers. He further observed:

> I have never believed in measuring the effectiveness of different campaigns. It would be impossible for us to separate and measure the impact of individual campaigns and promotional initiatives. I believe that the collective impact should be reflected through the premiums that we are able to get on our products in B2C situations. We also learnt that the expenditure on measurement of effectiveness turns out to be much more than the expenses incurred on the promotions and campaigns. We also discovered that measuring effectiveness can also lead you to a trap of getting the effectiveness measurement done by outsiders on every three or six months. For all these reasons, we believe in using our common sense and direct measures like increasing in share, sales and premiums and share of mind.

The VP continued:

> For B2B customers like Toyota and Hyundai; getting business from them is more important than price. These customers would always expect price parity or some discount. But the gain is the regularity of business. This happens because of consistency in performance and stability in our commercial dealings, i.e., part of contract management. Unlike our local competitors, Tata Steel does not change the price as and when the market situation changes. We have stuck to the contractual prices agreed for a specified period of time. Our customers like it. Only after the lapse of contract period, we have re-negotiated for the price revisions. Customer value management, and managing customer engagements and contract management for long term relationship, are seemingly working well for our B2B customers.

Brands provide easy entry on toll roads and gains are substantial

A CEO of a company of air compressors, feels that brand is definitely a critical aspect of B2B markets. But connotations would differ between B2C and B2B brands. In his opinion, while a strong B2C brand can help in enhancing sales and profitability, the same could not be true for B2B brands. A strong brand helps in an easy entry even when customers are new. But for this, the brand has to score high on trustworthiness.

As the CEO explained, air compressors are low value capital equipments. These have a very broad customer base. An efficient distribution network and a strong brand help. In fact a strong brand helps in getting strong distributors. It helps distributors earn premium and increase profits. It also helps the company to attract talent. For attracting talent, coverage in neutral media helps. So when his company gets covered by magazines and newspapers, it lends credibility to the company's image. Strong brand also helps in getting potential partners for the overseas business.

Reflecting on the performance of his organization, he shared:

> We have always been a service led organization. We have never entered into any mud slinging arguments with the customers. The customer satisfaction has been always high for our products. This has been a very strong underpinning for our brand. In last 6 to 7 years, we have spent lot of time in improving the product performance. Lot of time and effort has gone in designing and improving the products. This has changed the way customers are perceiving us. This too has had positive rub off onour Brand.

Reacting to a question of creating a brand driven business, the CEO commented: 'Brand is business may be true to a certain extent. But for us technology is the key. It's only the technology which would help us to maintain the strength of the brand.' Reflecting deeper, he felt: 'Brand could be a focal point. Value of brand starts increasing, when it begins getting linked to the segments which themselves start growing. Over the years, segments have polarized and have become large in our context.'

A strong brand in B2B markets can give easy entry, but it may not help in closing the sales. In the case of B2C, a strong brand helps in closing the sales. For B2C products like biscuits, one may have 10 segments. Each could be huge. These kinds of possibilities (in terms of size) are not present for capital goods like air compressors. But for consumables like lubricant and greases, scaling possibilities do exist. Due to this brand-building possibilities are always there for such kinds of products.

The CEO also observed that traditional methods of brand building have exhausted themselves. Unless one touches the whole envelope, the gains would not be there:

Initially, the travel on the trodden paths appears more seductive. But the new path, though less travelled, would ultimately lead to destination which would be very superior to what one can achieve through conventional 'run of the mill' kind of brand building approach. The challenge is how to deliver the whole experience to our customers, and suppliers.

Networking would be needed to sustain the leadership

Usha Martin Industries (UMI) Limited began its journey in 1962. By 1990s it had become an undisputed leader in steel wire ropes. Starting as a wire rope manufacturer, it expanded its operation through a series of backward integrations. By 2009, UMI had become a highly integrated mini steel plant for special grade steel with annual capacity of producing 0.4 million tonnes of steel. It owned its own iron ore mines, sponge iron units, mini blast furnace, wire rods mills and finally, wires and wire ropes. Commenting on its performance, the Chairman felt that UMI's unique model—iron ore to end products—has given competitive advantage and leadership. Over the years, through acquisitions and green field projects in Thailand, the UK, the USA and Dubai, UMI has become a global organization. It is exporting wire ropes to more than 150 countries. It has also set up four global service centres to serve the ships. By 2008, UMI's sales were around Rs 24,000 million. Out of these, steel wire rods contributed Rs 12,000 million, wire ropes accounted for Rs 10,000 million and jelly-filled cables accounted for Rs 2,000 million. Besides the 'steel' business, UMI also had an IT software business.

Wire ropes have multiple uses like in cranes, elevators, haulage and ships. Besides providing the function of lifting or moving, it also has to ensure safety of equipment and people. The wire rope from a manufacturer like UMI has to enjoy an image of strong and safe brand.

When asked whether 'brand' and 'branding' have any importance for products like wire ropes and wire rods, a cryptic comment of the Chairman was:

Its very crucial and important to become number one player. We have to put in substantial effort in brand building. This is needed to create global awareness and recognition. This would require convergence of several players of the value network, to make UMI a strong brand. It has to be sustained orchestrating of several partners of the network.

As he shared, in the past UMI was busy in stabilizing its financial performance, strengthening innovations and its R&D efforts and strengthening the talent base. It was his view that these efforts have helped substantially in making UMI a strong brand in India. But in spite of being the leader in wire ropes in India and the Number Two player globally, the Chairman felt that it has now reached a stage where UMI has to think of a fresh set of dedicated efforts in making UMI a global brand.

The Chairman felt that 'customers' visit to plant' is a very important ingredient in building strong B2B brands.

For a small customer base we do not need any brand building

Wipro Hydraulic System, Bangalore, is a Rs 16,000 million (as in 2008) company. It is part of the US$ 4 billion Wipro group which is the third largest computer software company of India. When asked about the brand-building initiative of his company, the MD counterd the question by saying: What brand building? They have just 11 customers. For this they do not need to spend money in any brand building. He also said for them relationship-building is more important. Though his corporate group had spend around Rs 400 million, i.e, around 1 per cent of sales in 2007, for the MD, performance and customer service were two most critical ingredients for a strong brand.

Strong brand is relationship management and extended credit terms

Lark Group deals in copper wires. It had a sale of around Rs 1,000 million in 2007. Its customer base of wires could be 20 large electrical appliances and machinery producers of India. It also sells to the traders of copper wires. 'What brand?' was the question asked by the CEO. He also said they need to manage relationship for their kind of business. Seemingly nothing of brand building and reaping a payoff came to his mind. When pushed further as to why customers come back to him, the response was quality, delivery, credit (nearly 90–100 days) and service. When asked to explain the aspect of service, he shared that besides the issues of logistics, the other dimension of the service was relationship management in several forms.

Brand is providing value added services

Till June 2009, Bushen Raina was the MD of the largest tinplate manufacturing company, TCIL, Jamshedpur. He remained at this position for over 13 years. Tinplate is used in producing metal containers. TCIL's total customer base may be around 300. Nearly 25 customers may account for 80 per cent of sales. Metal containers are used to package food products, milk powder, milk additives like Bournvita, Horlicks, and so on. The other end uses are for crown caps for cold drinks and beer bottles. Tinplate, once the most versatile packaging media till the late 1970s, is currently facing stiff competition from several substitutes like plastics, glass, laminates, aluminum, paper board and the like. Due to heavy in-roads by substitutes, tinplate and TCIL have faced very tough challenges to keep the business going and remain profitable. For Bushen, managing brand was to provide value added services to its customer. This included setting up a solution centre at Jamshedpur. This solution centre provides lacquered and printed tinplates and new shapes and types for the metal. When asked about his views on brands for a product like tinplate, he felt it is very important and observed that TCIL needs to learn a lot in brand-building activities. In the last 8–10 years, TCIL has played a very active role in promoting tinplate as a green product. For this the company has developed several innovative campaigns.

For strong brands customer's experience and internal allignment is very important

When asked as to what he understands by B2B brands, the Executive-in-Charge of Tata Tubes's (with sales of Rs 20,000 million in 2008) first observation was: 'I have often wondered whether there can be anything like B2B brand.' But in the very next observation he mentioned:

> Contractors and Airport Authority of India, always mentioning the brand of tubes like Tata or Jindal. A water conveyance tube is like a 'commodity' product. The institutional customers can buy any make of the tube once it conforms to the standard specifications. Why then they specify only two or three known brands? This gives the hint—brands do play in the mind of the buyers.

But beyond a product brand, he felt it is the 'corporate brand' which seemingly plays more important-cum-critical role for B2B customers. Thus, for furniture, customers would like to buy Godrej. This is due to Godrej being a strong corporate brand. But for products more complex than furniture and tubes, the Executive-in-Charge felt that brands cannot be built only through promotion and creating awareness. Strong brands are built on performance and relationships. He opined that in the context of B2B markets, customer experience is very important. The perception of brand grows through experiences. The low communications spend in B2B situations should not be construed as low concern for building and creating strong brands. For B2B brands, the time and effort put in relationship building, in R&D spends, in aligning the whole organization towards customers should be included in the cost of brand building. In this sense, the 'Ad' spend should include time and money spent in maintaining relationships with the customers. Continuing, he felt:

> 'Brand' is the way we do our business. This should be consistent with all the stake holders. This consistency may be missing in case of several entrepreneurs. If this is absent, it would be difficult for them to build a strong brand. In case of Tatas, the blue 'T' logo is sufficient to convey a sense of trust and confidence. Buyers do not have to check the ethics and morals of a company associated with the house of Tatas. The brand becomes the person who is marketing the brand.
>
> Brand in B2B context should be both for internal and external customers. I was shocked to discover that 600 out of a workforce of 1,200 had not even known our 'Structura' brand for buildings and structures. We are now making an extra effort to let our entire workforce know about Structura. If they do not know what we are doing, we would never be able to align them towards our brand building process. This may reflect in our inability to maintain consistency in all the situations.

Preference more than the premium should be the key contribution of a strong brand

The VP of Electrical Switchgear Products (ESP) of L&T along with the team of six senior executives feels that brand has a very important role to play even for B2B products like circuit breakers, switch fuses, starters, electrical metres, electrical relays, and so on. Due to its strong brand, L&T has been able to get premium. 'But before premiums, "preference by customers" was the key contribution of strong brands', and it was an equivocal opinion for the entire group. The group felt that 'people' behind the product make the difference in creating a strong and positive perception. Consistency in customer policies creates a strong brand. As the group observed: 'Our customers feel that L&T would never leave them in lurch, no matter when the product was purchased.' L&T has created this trust over the years. L&T has taken care to ensure that whosoever interacts with the customers would reinforce this trust and commitment. The group shared that for several decades, ESP had only two segments. These were agriculture (motor starters for farmers) and industries. In both these segments, L&T has maintained its leadership. The use of its products could enable the electrical panel manufacturers to gain customer confidence and easy acceptance. Besides right policies, high quality human resource and a sense of assurance to the customers, ESP has also believed in creating a strong brand by maintaining close relationship with specifiers, consultants and architects. The group shared:

Over the years, the competitive scenario has changed in India. Our competitors are now well established global giants. But we are making conscious efforts to tell the specifiers that we are home grown, good and more reliable than the MNCs. We are trying to create differentiation by highlighting the advantages of dealing with us. Flexibility in adapting to the specific needs, making service and spares available through our strong service network are the key differentiators which our MNC competitors would not be able to match in India.

It said further:

When MNCs drop a design, they not only deprive the customers of the spares but do not even care to share their decisions to withdraw products. On the other hand, we inform our customers well in advance.

Our customers, by now, know that irrespective of the good or bad business situation, we have always been honest and open. Our strategy to create new segments from 2 to 5 and to enhance our global presence is demanding new brand building initiatives. For global markets, MNCs have an advantage. But in the last 10 years, we have been able to bridge the gap between the premium which foreign brands used to get. Thus when we entered the markets of Middle East, we had given discounts as high as 30% to get orders. But over the same last 10 years, the gap has come down. The MNCs are now able to get only 25% premium from us. In India, the MNCs are unable to enjoy this premium. In fact, we have been able to improve our market share from 40% to 50% in India. This is because L&T is synonymous with quality and reliability in India. All these are rewards for building the products of ESP [Electrical Switchgear Products] as power brands. But for global markets, except for the Middle East, we are not there in any markets. Our manufacturing base in China would help us to enhance our global presence and performance. But our brand building efforts would vary from country to country.

The group felt that both product and company brand-building work in tandem. The strong corporate brand of L&T has definitely helped. Another effort of L&T was to win awards. It won the Best Electrical Panel Building award from GE Capital and the Best Manufacturer award from Sloan School of Management, USA. These too have helped in brand building.

The group also felt that besides three training centres (located in Pune, Lucknow and Coonoor), 100 authorized service centres and its R&D set up at Powai have contributed immensely in brand building. Similarly, customers visit to manufacturing facilities is a very effective way to build strong brands.

The Evolutionary Nature of Branding Challenges: The Telcon Experience

Telcon: Telco Construction Equipment Company Ltd— A Tata–Hitachi joint venture

During the course of my research, I came across a very interesting experience of Telcon, a leader in construction equipment of India.

Despite being part of the house of Tatas with an existence for nearly 10 years and having a team of very capable professionals, it is faced with branding challenges because of rapid growth in multiple produce lines. It is not that the management is not aware of the importance of brands for its business; the development of managing its growth seems to be unleashing never ending branding challenges. Several reasons seem to have contributed to this situation. One was the very vast range of products. These included excavators, dumpers, wheeled equipment, road-making equipment, crawler cranes, all terrain cranes, hydraulic cranes and some more. The second reason was the acquisition of two companies in Spain in 2007. This has not only widened the product mix, but also the markets beyond India. Post acquisition, Rana Sinha, MD of Telcon, and his group were keen to embark on a robust and sustained brand building campaign for Telcon. This demanded clarity and decisions in several areas. But the historical evolution of Telcon as an entity was preventing easy and straightforward decisions.

Telcon came into being in 1999. It is a joint venture promoted by Tata Motors (holding 60 per cent of the shares) and Hitachi Construction Machinery Company Limited, Japan (with 40 per cent share). Hitachi was amongst the top five construction equipments companies in the world. By 2007, Telcon ranked 47th in the world. It has a vision to be amongst the top 25 global player by 2012. The ambitious targets of rapid growth to achieve a sales turnover of US$ 2 billion needed strong brands within and outside India.

By 2007, it was supplying around 10,000 machines per annum from its two factories in Jamshedpur and Dharwar (Karnataka). Telcon's customer base was around 15,000 for nearly 43,000 machines. By 2009, its sales had reached 0.7 billion.

A senior executive shared that for construction equipments, product brand recall was more important than corporate brand. The customer would always recall products by their brand name and numbers like Tata–Hitachi EX-200 in the Hydraulic Excavator Business and Tata 3036 in the wheel loader line, and so on. For this reason too, Rana and his team were keen to have clarity in the product branding decisions.

Telcon's diary for 2010 listed several product categories. Each product had different brand names. These included brands like Tata Hitachi excavators, Tata TWL 3036 wheel loaders, Hitachi Sumitomo Crawler Cranes, AR 2000 (road resurfacing equipment), Telcon Serviplem Transit Mixers, and many more.

At the time of formation of Telcon in 1999, its management had several choices to brand its product range. One alternative was to use 'Tata' as an umbrella brand for its entire product range. The other choice was to develop hyphenated brands like Tata–Hitachi Excavators and the like. Even though the name 'Tata' could provide trust and assurance, the management argued, Telcon would have lost the advantage of not using 'Hitachi' in its brands. Even before the formation of Telcon, Tata Motors had collaboration with Hitachi (since 1984) to manufacture construction equipment. It had named these excavators as Tata–Hitachi. Compared to Tata and Hitachi which were very powerful brand names, Telcon was a lesser known brand. But having named the company as Telcon, Rana and his team were keen to use 'Telcon', besides using the names of 'Tata' and 'Hitachi'. Rana's marketing team was of the view that brand recall played a very critical role in repeat business. Every product required a brand name. By 2008, Telcon had 11 sub-brands. Their inability to use 'Telcon' for several products was causing uneasiness in the team. Most major global players such as CAT, Komatsu and VOLVO operate with unique brand identities while some such as TEREX use multiple hyphenated brands.

Over the years, Tata–Hitachi had become a major selling point for the sales people. The brand recall was very high for Tata–Hitachi. Similarly the backhoe loader originally under the brand name of Tata–JohnDeere (erstwhile collaborator) had achieved high recall amongst the customers.

In 2005, Hitachi acquired 40 per cent stake in Telcon. At this point of time, the management was debating to rename Telcon as 'Tata–Hitachi Construction Equipment Company'. If this had happened, Telcon as a name would have ceased to exist. But this proposal did not find favour with other Director of Tata Motors and

Tata Sons. They insisted on continuing with 'Telcon' as the name of the company as attaching 'Hitachi' to it could eliminate chances of joining up with other construction equipment majors in future. This issue lingered from 2005 till end of 2007. Once resolved, it became imperative for Rana and his team to think of strategy and plans to build 'Telcon' as a brand. Between the interim period of two years, i.e., between 2005 and 2007, the Telcon team was emphasizing on 'Tata–Hitachi' as the brand-building platform in the hydraulic excavator business in which Telcon is the market leader

But by the time the issue of 'Telcon' vs 'Tata–Hitachi' was resolved (i.e., by the end of 2007), Telcon acquired two companies in Spain. Each had strong presence and awareness in their served markets. This created another branding challenge for Rana and his team—the brand names of Ready Mix Concrete Mixers and pumps of Serviplem, both in India and abroad. Baryval of Serviplem was a very strong brand in Europe for concrete transit mixers and pumps. But the same was not true for India. In India, Ready Mix Concrete (RMC), a brand from the UK, belonged to the Rahejas. Schewing Stetter of Germany and Greaves were other well-known brands for RMC equipments in India. Telcon had a choice to either build 'Baryval' in India or develop a new brand like Tata–Baryval or Tata–Telcon–Baryval as a brand for India and global markets. Similar was the need for the Lebrero range of road construction equipment the other Spanish company acquired by Telcon.

The struggle for Rana and his team to have one unified brand for all equipments seems to have become a never-ending race. This is evident from the two calendars I received from Telcon for the year 2010. A calendar with a theme of climate change has a very visible attempt to highlight the logo of Telcon with two taglines for Tata—Leadership with Trust—and Hitachi—Inspire the Next. The other is the Hitachi calendar showing equipments with Hitachi's tagline—'Reliable Solutions'—on the top and Telcon's tagline—'Constructive Solutions'—at the bottom. Its association with the house of Tata is missing. To an outsider like me, the entire brand-building effort appears to be diffused, highly cluttered and fragmented. But the solution does not appear to be easy either!

Summing Up

After reading this chapter it should become clear that the idea of 'brand' and 'branding' is not as straightforward for B2B markets as it is for B2C markets. To a large extent, the nature of the product, industry and end use situations would determine the importance and task for creating B2B brands.

Executives contacted were either CEOs or MDs of their organizations. In spite of the diversity of products—refractories, flat steel products, wire ropes, air compressors, hydraulic systems, tinplate, ESPs, steel tubes and copper wires—all are hardcore B2B products, none seem to have underplayed on the importance of B2B brands. In fact for a large majority of the leaders, identification of several new and innovative ways to strengthen their brands would remain a challenge.

Creating Corporate Brands: The Key Asset of any B2B Brand

Introduction

The corporate brand is like the soul, while the company is a bit like the body. The corporate brand lives on, even if the body changes.

—Gopalakrishnan, Executive Director,
Tata Sons, quoted by Chacko (2005)

As per Gregory (2004: 3):

It is not an ad campaign, a logo, a spokesperson, or a slogan. Rather, a corporate brand is the product of the millions of experiences a company creates—with employees, vendors, investors, reporters, communities, and customers—and the emotional feelings these groups develop as a result.

This gets reflected in the brand equity valuations. It is one intangible resource which cannot be copied by anyone. It is the face of any organization that people will first see. It is deeply entrenched in the mind of customers which tilts the decision in favour of the company enjoying a strong brand image even when everything appears similar.

But brands and branding would make sense only when the firm's performance is sustained over decades or even centuries. A firm's performance is an outcome of decisions taken over the years covering what Ansoff (1965: 1–11) had suggested in strategic, administrative and operational areas. Strengthening of brands would require investments and innovation in technology, processes, people and programmes. The impact has to be coherent and cohesive.

The three chapters in this part contain stories of three great corporate brands from India: Tata, L&T and Infosys. To me, if not in size, in terms of sales and market caps as compared to the frequently mentioned GE, IBM, Microsoft, Intel and some more companies, these well-known Indian brands would match on all parameters of creating and managing great brands.

Russi Lala (2004) in his book *For the Love of India* had shared: 'If wishes could work, the streets of India could be paved with the gold.' Taking a clue from him, I wish to add that if fanciful promotions and branding activities could work, every company or firm could have become a great brand. Unfortunately 'branding' alone cannot make great brands. Thus, it took nearly 89 billion (Jagannathan 2002) worth of investment 1983 onwards and a massive dose of processes, management, tools and techniques sustained over nearly 20 years to make Tata Steel the lowest cost producer of steel in the world. Tata Steel has been promoting its brand for long. But mere communications, without strategic interventions in modernizing and upgrading the technology, would have failed to provide world-class products at competitive prices. Tata Steel's actions are in line with what Kotler and Keller (2006: 273) have suggested: 'Building a strong brand requires careful planning and a great deal of long term investment. At the heart of a successful brand is a great product or service, backed by creatively designed and executed marketing.'

After reading the story of these three great brands, readers should feel rejuvenated to achieve their dreams and aspirations.

4

If you have not got a brand, you have not got a business.

—Anonymous

~~~   ~~~

Customers must recognize that you stand for something.

—Harvard Schultz Starbucks

4

Brand Tata: Leadership with Trust

When you have to give the lead in action, in ideas—a lead which does not fit in with the very climate of opinion—that is true courage, physical or mental or spiritual, call it what you like, and it is this type of courage and vision that Jamsetji Tata showed. It is right that we should honour his memory and remember him as one of the big founders of modern India.

—Jawaharlal Nehru, first Prime Minister of India, quoted by Lala (1992: 3)

The wealth gathered by Jamsetji Tata and his sons in half a century of industrial pioneering formed but a minute fraction of the amount by which they enriched the nation. The whole of that wealth is held in trust for the people and used exclusively for their benefit. The cycle is thus complete. What came from the people has gone back to the people many times over.

—J.R.D. Tata, CEO, Tata Sons (1938–91)[1]

Born in 1867 and Still Young

There is no precise date to signify the birth of the Tata Group, but a loose marker could be 1867, the year in which a 28-year-old Jamsetji Tata established the trading firm Tata and Sons. That was the modest beginning of a brand that is today valued in billions of dollars. (Chacko 2005)

Thousands of articles and hundreds of books may fail to capture the creation of the most revered brand of India. This chapter, in this sense, would be a mere tribute. Yet, I am keen to share with the readers—may be in small bits and pieces—as to how a great brand, which was born in 1867, is young, strong and vibrant even after 140 years.

By 2008, the sales revenue of the Tata group of companies had reached US$ 65 billion. Nearly 65 per cent (US$ 38 billion) was from the global operations. It was operating in 80 countries, had a workforce of 0.3 million plus people and a market cap of US$ 52 billion (Brand Finance Global 500 2009). Brand Finance, a UK-based consultancy firm, in early January 2009, had valued the Tata brand at US$ 11.4 billion. It was ranked 51st amongst the top 100 brands of the world. As per Brand Finance, Tata was the only brand from India to come in top 100 (Brand Finance Global 500 2009). Similarly *Business Week* (2008) ranked the group the sixth amongst the 'World's most innovative companies' and the Reputation Institute of the USA (2008) rated it as the 'World's sixth most reputed firm in the world in early 2008'. Like this, the list of awards would be very long indicating the vibrancy and achievement of the house of Tata and its business and non-business organizations.

Its business interest includes 106 companies.[2] Out of the 106 companies, the majority would be operating predominantly in B2B markets. These include companies like Tata Steel, Tata Motors, Tata Consultancy Services (TCS), Tata Chemicals, Tata Tea Limited, India Hotels, Tata Power Limited, Tata Communication and many more. Barring a few, each company has been a leader for long in its chosen field.

House of Tata: A Confederation of Companies

When asked as to how you would define the house of Tata and what links the companies together, J.R.D. Tata, who had been the CEO of the company for more than 53 years observed:

> I would call it a group of individually managed companies united by two factors. First a feeling that they are part of a larger group which carries the name and prestige of Tatas and public recognition of honesty and reliability—trust-worthiness. They use the Tata emblem. The reason is, you might say, enlightened self-interest. The other reason is more metaphysical. There is innate loyalty, a sharing of certain beliefs. We all feel a certain pride that we are somewhat different from others. This factor has also worked against our growth. What would have happened if our philosophy

was like that of some other companies which do not stop at any means to attain their ends. I have often thought of that and I have come to the conclusion that if we were like other groups, we would be twice as big as they are today. What we have sacrificed is a 100 per cent growth, but we wouldn't want it any other way. (Lala 1992: 225)

What seems to come out is that till the time J.R.D. was the CEO of the house of Tatas, it was a confederation of several companies tied together with Tata beliefs, values and purpose. These purpose and practices are still holding the group even after 140 years. The strongest driver amongst its values and purpose, according to me, are the words of J.R.D. which are as follows: 'Nothing is worth attempting that would not benefit the Nation' (Lala 2007: xiv).

The J.N. Tata Legacy: A Unique Heritage of Brand Tata

Men of business are not often at home in the world of ideas; it was Jamsetji's distinction that he lived in both worlds—the world of ideas and the world of action.

—J.R.D. Tata[3]

Jamshetji Nusserwanji Tata (1839–1904) is still the most visible icon of brand Tata. Every year on 3 March, Tata Steel celebrates its Founder's Day, the birth date of J.N. Tata. To mark the occasion, there is a very colourful ceremony involving a parade, floats, dances and illuminations in the night. But leading the entire ceremony are the old employees, some even 90 years old, raising slogan such as 'Tata Maharaj ki Jai' (Long Live Tata) and eager to garland his statue. The reverence of this very large family of the house of Tata is not confined to Jamshedpur. It is there in Mithapur of Tata Chemicals or in Khapoli of Tata Hydro Power and in several other places.

His legacy is widely shared and stored in thousands of articles and hundreds of books. Amongst all the Indian business persons, even till 2009, no one is remembered in a similar manner as J.N. Tata. Russi Lala,[4] author of many books on the house of Tata, felt that J.N. Tata's ethos was rooted in his community and its faith—Zorastrianism. As he explains the essence of Zorastrianism is simple: '*Humata* (Good Thoughts), *Hukta* (Good Words), *Huvasta* (Good Deeds)'. Commenting further, Lala observed that it was not accidental that he adopted this maxim as his motto.

Such was the power of his passion to build India and also a great organization for the good of the society that it prompted Mahatma Gandhi to observe: 'Tatas represent the Spirt of Adventure' (Lala 2004: 154). And while inaugurating the Jubilee Park—a gift to the town in 1958, i.e., the golden jubilee year of Tata Steel—Nehru, the first Prime Minister of India said: 'I wish India had 500 Jamshedpurs' (Lala 2007: 151). Pandit Nehru, the creator of modern India, was also looking for a role model to accelerate the growth and development of India. To him, Jamshedpur appeared an ideal to emulate. He was paying rich tribute to its founder, J.N. Tata and those managing the house of Tatas post J.N. Tata's death.

When he was busy getting clearances for his projects like setting up a steel plant, hydel power station and a university of advanced research, he was seemingly not aware that he was also planting the seed for a strong brand that would manifest itself without indulging in any explicit brand-building activities.

> The soul of the Tata corporate brand has been expressed down the ages through an exceptional set of qualities: consistency, single-mindedness, openness and credibility. Add to these factors such as caring for the wider community and helping in the construction of national resources, and you get a marque that is almost unique.

These are words of Gopalakrishnan, Executive Director, Tata Sons, and the main architect of the branding initiatives of Tata Sons. He calls this a phenomenon of *swayambhu*, the self-manifested—a term Sanskrit scholars use for the divine miracle (Agrawal 2007). These words almost echo the views of some scholars who feel that great brands just happen, they can never be created.

Commenting upon the distinctiveness, Dr J.J. Irani, Director, Tata Sons and ex-MD of Tata Steel feels: 'In India, and increasingly in some other parts of the world, a Tata calling card evokes instant recognition and respect. The quality and values that the Tata marque stands for are also the characteristics of a true-blue Tata person' (Irani 2008).

Ratan Tata's Initiatives: One Strong Brand vs 40 Brands

In spite of commitment to the Tata ethos and business leadership of individual companies, the brand Tata was lacking a collective and unified effort till 1992, i.e., when Mr Ratan Tata became the Chairman of the group. Recognizing the reality, he spearheaded the brand-building initiatives of the group. The goal was to unify a diverse and diffused enterprise to make it capable of facing the post-liberalization challenges from well-known global companies. In an interview with *The Economic Times* in 1996, Ratan Tata stressed the importance of constructing a unified Tata brand:

> The intention has been to create a single strong entity that will benefit all Tata companies If you are to fight a Mitsubishi or an X or Y in the free India of tomorrow, you better have one rather than 40 brands. You better have the ability to promote that brand in a meaningful manner. (*The Economic Times* 1996)

Though convincing the CEOs of various companies was easy, implementation to ensure a unified approach was a major challenge. The mechanism thought was a creation of a concept: Brand Equity and Business Promotion (BEBP). The plan was two-fold. One was to urge companies to follow the conditions and guidelines for using the Tata brand name. The other was to raise funds to manage the Tata brand. In the final scheme of things, each company signs the agreement with Tata Sons—the owner of Tata, the brand. Companies have the choice not to sign the agreement, but in such case they would lose the right to use the name of Tata. By 2009, Tata Brand Equity Fund had the support of 100 group companies. As shared by a senior executive of the house of Tata, these companies use the Tata brand name, like Tata Steel and Tata Motors, and contribute 0.25 per cent of sales or 0.5 per cent of profit before tax, whichever is less. While others like Voltas and Rallis contribute 0.15 per cent of their sales. The Fund is used to finance the group's brand-building exercise within and outside the country. With most of the Tata group companies growing aggressively, the corpus of this fund is expected to be substantial.

The New Logo of Brand Tata

Parallel to putting the BEBP initiative in motion, the group acquired a fresh and modern logo developed by the British design agency Wolff Olins. This logo is now used by the group companies who contribute to the brand equity fund, and have agreed to implement the Tata Business Excellence Model (TBEM). In the last decade, the new logo has become a powerful symbol of brand Tata. This has provided a strong umbrella to all the group companies.

Brand Tata's Repositioning: The Initial Phase

The roll-out plan was a well thought through plan. It began with the 'perception survey' conducted by A.C. Nielson in 1999. It revealed that whereas the Tata brand was perceived to be a large, profitable, established and caring, it did not appear as a strong, focused and modern brand. To the majority, it appeared as a 'laidback leader'. These almost corroborated with the perceptions and beliefs the top management had about the brand Tata. The survey also vindicated the long held beliefs about brand Tata. Some of these were (Agrawal 2007):

- Brand Tata would never cheat.
- It would follow practices which could face the public scrutiny.
- Would be compassionate towards society and humanity.
- Would not deviate from the legacy of its founder.

The management felt that 'Leadership with Trust' could be a legitimate claim of brand Tata, but at the same time it appeared weak on 'action'. The brand, to outsiders, appeared low on vibrancy and vitality.

This led to the re-articulation of the aspirations for repositioning of the brand without losing its heritage and deep rooted core values of the house of Tatas. The management wanted the new brand Tata to appear youthful and attract top quality managers who could help brand Tata to recast and sustain future business leadership.

The Implementations: Challenges of Size, Diversity and Legacy

The power of a unified approach to build a strong, new brand Tata was easy to comprehend, but to achieve alignment of all the 106 units needed adherence to frameworks which could provide both endurance and performance without compromising with the ethical standards of the group. The group conceived of two initiatives to achieve excellence and integrity. One was the introduction of the J.R.D. Tata Business Excellence Model or TBEM (on the lines of famous Malcolm Baldrige award of the US) for corporate leadership and the other was the development of Tata code of conduct to ensure integrity and honesty in behaviour and practices of its enterprises and executives.

An outside agency was hired to develop the 'Rule Book' and also the standards to ensure a proper use of brand properties like signages, colours, do's and don'ts, etc.

Some Specific Branding Initiatives

An important concern of the repositioning exercise was to change the image of brand Tata to appear more dynamic, youthful and zestful. The management felt the new brand, instead of a domineering personality of a mentor, should appear a combination of all three equally domineering characteristics. These were the characteristics of a mentor, fighter and winner.

It was felt that the association with winners in sports would not only change brand imagery, but also appear contemporary to younger people. The events thought and sponsored were Tata Open Tennis, Tata Racing (with Narain Karthikeya, first ever Formula 1 racer from India) and musical concerts by Bob Dylan, Sharon Prabhakar and Zubin Mehta. Knowledge events were organized in association with *India Today* (The India Today Conclave) and *Indian Express* (The Indian Empowered series). The other sets of events included were the 'Tata Crucible Business Quiz' for young executives, 'Tata Crucible Campus Quiz' for B-school and engineering students and 'Tata Building India Essay Contest' for schoolchildren. All these activities and events were an attempt to make brand Tata appear as a balanced combination of 'fighter, mentor and winner'.

For the year 2004, which was the centenary year of J.N. Tata's death, an additional attraction was a formal exhibition which chronicled the history and achievements of the group. This exhibition travelled to 11 cities across India and also to countries like South Africa, Singapore and Korea.

Tracking the Change

An important part of the brand-building initiative has been the 'track' studies conducted by outside research agencies. This is done twice a year. Round six of the track was completed in July 2003. By July 2009, 17 rounds were over. These track studies have been measuring the brand performance of brand Tata with some other well-known Indian corporate brands (see Table 4.1).

Besides measurement on the multiple parameters, the track studies were also assessing the brand performance on two dimensions of 'affinity' and 'relevance'. (A brand leader is one who is high on affinity as well as relevance.) The track studies indicate that brand Tata has sustained its position as a leader. In fact, as

Table 4.1   The Brand Parameters Used in the Track Studies

Former Studies	Recent Studies
1. Knowledge of the business environment	1. Vision and focus
2. Dynamism	2. Diversification
3. Work place quality	3. Reputed and well known
4. Quality of product and services	4. Dynamism and Innovation
5. Consistency and dependability of quality	5. Employee focus
6. Reputation	6. Ethical and social responsibility
7. Renown	7. Financial soundness
	8. Quality conscious and responses

Source: Interviews with Tata Steel's executives.

claimed by the management (Agrawal 2007) it is the only brand that has consistently consolidated its position; the other comparative companies have seen ups and downs in their leadership.

Commenting on the success of the repositioning of brand, Gopalakrishnan observed (Agrawal 2007):

> While its old-world properties remain unaltered, the Tata brand has moved on to conquer new turf. Today it is increasingly being seen as innovative, forward thinking, well managed and aggressive. With high technology content in the product quality, it has right ingredients for prosperity.

Brand Tata Going Global: Actions and Challenges

> We have two guiding arrows. One points overseas, where we want to expand markets for our existing products. The other points right here, to India, where we want to explore the large mass market that is emerging—not by following but by breaking new ground in product development and seeing how we can do something that hasn't been done before.
>
> —Ratan Tata, Group Chairman

Tata Exports, which was set up in 1962 and later became Tata International, was the group's first attempt to unify the exports from group companies. Its export sales in 2007 were around US$ 850 million. In spite of the desire to unify, several large group of companies continued to maintain their independent exports. Even by 2009, most of the companies were still exporting independently. The key difference, 1999 onwards, has been the adoption of the common 'T' logo of the house of Tatas.

As claimed by Tata Sons websites, its major companies are now beginning to be counted globally. Tata Steel became the sixth largest steel maker in the world after the acquisition of Corus. Tata Motors is amongst the top five commercial vehicle manufacturers in the world. In early 2008, it acquired two famous brands, Jaguar and Land Rover. Tata Tea is the second largest branded tea company in the world along with its UK-based subsidiary, Tetley. Tata Chemicals is the world's second largest manufacturer of soda ash. TCS is one of the leading global software business companies with delivery centres in the US, the UK, Hungary, Brazil, Uruguay and China, apart from India. But in spite of a plethora of globalization activities, as a senior executive Peter Unsworth, Tetley's Chief Operating Officer observed: 'It will take hundreds of millions of pounds of investment to make Tata a household name' (Singh 2008). He shared that he has been often asked by colleagues about the possibility of printing Tata brand on Tetley packaging (Tata tea had acquired Tetley in 2005 at a cost of US$ 407 million. But till January 2008, Tetley was not disclosing the identity of its owners, i.e., Tatas).

Gopalakrishnan, Executive Director of Tata Sons agrees (Singh 2008): 'Brand building and producing babies are similar—you cannot accelerate the nine months by putting more doctors, gynaecologists and nurses. Similarly, brands will evolve and grow in a certain way and it will take time.' He also observed:

It would be unwise, at present, to launch a $100-million programme around the world to establish the Tata name because we are not an IBM or a GE, whose brand represents a single product genre. We have multiple product categories in multiple geographies, all of which do not overlap. So we have to build our brand in chosen geographies. We are at the juncture now where we are looking at how we can go about significantly expanding our global brand promotion. (Singh 2008)

An example illustrative of the Tata way of creating global brand is South Africa. It is a country where many Tata companies have already set up businesses, and others are looking at entering its market. The essence of the South Africa strategy is the three-circle approach: addressing leaders, influencers and journalists in three target groups—businesses, industries and the public. The communication is that Tata is a local company owned by an Indian group—a good corporate citizen. The South Africa Marketing Council has also jointly developed along with the Tata group a TV commercial welcoming the Tatas to the country and promoting Tata as a South African brand. Gopalakrishnan shared that a similar approach could be followed in the US, China and other countries where Tatas have substantial business activities. The branding strategies would, however, be adapted to suiting specific countries.

Reflecting on the challenges of globalization, Mr Anwar Hasan (Singh 2008), the London-based CEO of Tata Incorporate says: 'Brand Tata and Brand India have grown together in this market.' He furthers: 'When Tata Tea acquired Tetley, the popular perception was that Tetley was bought over by an Indian company. It was only after Corus that connecting the dots led to brand Tata.' To push the brand aggressively, the group has recently hired a public relations firm, Financial Dynamics, to build its brand through a multi-pronged programme in the UK market, targeting the media and other influencers.

Brand with a Societal Purpose: The Key Essence of Brand Tata

The Tata philosophy of management has always been and is today more than ever, that corporate enterprises must be managed not merely in the interests of their owners, but equally in those of their employees, of the customers of their products, of the local community and finally of the country as a whole.

—J.R.D. Tata[5]

Tata group has always believed in returning wealth to the society it serves. Two-thirds of the equity of Tata Sons is held by philanthropic trusts. These have created national institutions in science and technology, medical research, social studies and in performing arts. Contribution to social causes works out to nearly 8–14 per cent of the group's net profit. Each and every group company associated with brand Tata is alive to the needs of the society and their role in improving the quality of living. A long list of awards and recognition is a testimony to this glorious contribution. Even a selective pick is long:

- Tata Steel Ltd has been awarded the Golden Peacock Global Award for Corporate Social Responsibility (CSR) for the year 2009.

- Tata Chemicals set up the Tata Chemicals Society for Rural Development (TCSRD) in 1980 to promote its social uplift projects for communities in and around Mithapur (in the state of Gujarat in western India), Babrala (in the state of Madhya Pradesh in central India) and Haldia (in the state of West Bengal in eastern India).

- Rallilove ACTS (Assisting Communities through Service), an organization set up by Rallis, seeks to improve the quality of life of the poor, especially women and children, through sustainable community development programmes.

- Voltas for Women (VOW) was founded in 1965. The organization, whose membership is restricted to female employees of Voltas and wives of male employees, helps the needy with assistance in health and education, and offers career and vocational guidance.

- The second global Tata Interactive Systems Learning Disability Forum 2007 held in Mumbai sought to encourage, enable and empower all those who have to deal with learning disabilities on a day-to-day basis.

- Tata Power's unique CSR initiatives in Lonavala, Maharashtra, have created awareness about forest preservation and the environment, and have also provided employment opportunities to villagers living in the catchment areas of its dams.

- Instead of a handout, hold out a helping hand. That is the principle which enabled the Taj group to transform a group of ordinary Mumbai fisherwomen into a collective business enterprise. Instead of killing the vulnerable whale shark, fishermen on the Gujarat coast now protect it, thanks to an innovative campaign initiated by Tata Chemicals.

- The Tata group recognized the need to protect and conserve the world's natural resources long before it became a mantra of modern business. Tata companies are recycling and utilizing their waste in innovative ways.

- The Sir Ratan Tata Trust, together with the NGOs CInI and PRADAN, is helping tribals in Jharkhand strengthen their existing sources of livelihood and is also exploring new avenues for their development.

- Muskaan, with the help of the Sir Ratan Tata Trust, is rehabilitating children in urban slums of Bhopal through holistic, sustainable and collaborative initiatives.
- In 2006, TCS achieved the gold band for its performance in the Community Index with a score of 94.7 per cent. Known internationally for its business success, TCS has a warm spot in the heart of many Indians for the Computer-based Functional Literacy Project.

Brand with a Human Face

Economist Alfred Marshall had made the following observation in mid-1920: 'A score of Tatas might do more for India than any government, British or indigenous, can accomplish' (Gopalakrishnan 2004a).

Disasters and crisis are common occurrences in a country like India. The house of Tatas has set up Tata Relief Committee (TRC) to mobilize and provide relief work from its group companies in cases of major disasters like the Gujarat earthquake in 2001, Tsunami of 2004 or floods in Bihar in 2008. Each crisis required massive interventions to rehabilitate the victims on a permanent basis. These interventions go beyond the CSR activities of individual companies like Tata Steel and Tata Motors. For such crises the group philosophy is not to contribute in cash or kind through any agency, but to do something of a permanent nature, directly under the agies of TRC.

> Thus on 29 January 2001, Tata group Chairman appealed for donations to finance the work. TRC had begun. Employees of every Tata Company donated a day's salary each. Their respective companies then put in a matching contribution. The Sir Dorabji Tata Trust donated an amount of Rs 1.50 crore towards the TRC operations. The Corpus of TRC's relief and rehabilitation fund totalled Rs 9.37 crore. (Gandhy 2004)

TRC provided similar relief to rehabilitate victims of the Orissa cyclone, victims of Latur earthquake in 1993 and the major disaster of flooding of Chasnala (underground coal mines in 1970).

Why do Tata companies care so much? According to Branzei and Nadkarni (2008):

> The answer is: Because that is the Tata way—and because their employees are trusted (and expected) to approach their tasks and their volunteering with society in mind. They do not do something because it pays. They do it because it matters—to their business model, to their own development as leaders, and to the legacy their company wants to leave behind.

Brand Tata and Longevity

In one of his letters to his sons, J.N. Tata wrote:

> If you cannot make it greater, at least preserve it. Do not let things slide. Go on doing my work and increasing it, but if you cannot, do not lose what we have already done.[6]

Looking at the performance of the house of Tatas over 140 years, his sons and the vast team of 300 thousand plus professionals have seemingly done exceedingly well. Echoing this are the words of Ratan Tata:

> One hundred years from now, I expect the Tatas to be much bigger than it is now. More importantly, I hope the Group comes to be regarded as being the best in India—best in the manner in which we operate, best in the products we deliver and best in our value systems and ethics. Having said that, I hope that a hundred years from now we will spread our wings far beyond India ... (Branzei and Nadkarni 2008)

One is also keen to quote Arie de Geus' thoughts which Gopalakrishnan had shared in the speech delivered at the Northern Regional Convention 2004 organized by Allahabad Management Association on 13 March:

Arie de Geus wrote in *The Living Company*, that an economic company is like a puddle of rainwater—a collection of raindrops, gathered together in a cavity. The other type of company is organised around the purpose of perpetuating itself as an ongoing community. This type of company is like a river. It is turbulent because no drop of water remains in the same place for long, it finally flows out in the sea but the river lasts many times longer than the lifetime of the individual drops of water which comprise it. (Gopalakrishnan 2004b)

Tata river which began to flow around 1860s is still flowing and would continue to flow.

Long live the House of Tata!

5

We are citizens of a great country on the verge of bold advance, and we have to live upto that high standard.

—Jawaharlal Nehru

5

Brand L&T: Nation Building to Building Nations

> India, my adopted homeland, has a special place in my heart. With the Padma Bhushan, I am happy to realise that I have a place in her heart too.
>
> —Holck-Larsen on receiving the Padma Bhushan

L&T: A 'National Sector Private Company'

In a ceremony to commemorate 70 years of L&T's existence, and the birth centenary of Holck-Larsen on 21 December 2007, the chief guest, the then Finance Minister of India, Mr P. Chidambaram said:

> L&T is a unique company. Who owns it? We don't know. Institutions own it. Individuals own it and a trust of employees owns it. So in a sense, L&T does not belong to the public sector or the private sector. It really belongs to the nation. If we can carve out a sector called the National sector, I think L&T will be the first company to rank in that sector.[1]

The remark was greeted with applause from the audience comprising CEOs, heads of institutions and political leaders. The observation also brought to the fore a term that was distinctive and accurate in its description of L&T's unique status—a 'national sector company'.

The Beginning: Building India

Two Danish engineers Henning Holck-Larsen and Soren Toubro first visited India in 1936 as executives of FLSmidth—a Denmark-based cement manufacturer. Soon, they decided to strike out on their own and set up the eponymous partnership that was to have such a decisive influence on the Indian industry. Right from the formative years, the partners regarded national priorities as a road-map for the direction that their business would take. When World War II broke out, they turned adversity into opportunity and took the first step into manufacturing. Today, as Mr Chidambaram put it so eloquently, the company remains strongly committed to the country's larger goals. Although it has established its credentials as multinational—with a presence in more than 18 countries with a customer base in more than 40 countries and exports accounting for almost 20 per cent of total sales—its heart is still very much Indian. Reflecting his passion for India, Mr A.M. Naik, Chairman and MD of the company, opened his jubilee celebration speech by quoting from the company's much loved anthem. Translated into English, the lines say: 'We have to repay the debt to the soil which gave us birth.'

The Brand L&T: Living Its Own Vision

L&T's vision statement is widely displayed in every office—headquarters, regional offices and more than 300 construction sites in India and abroad. It reads:

L&T shall be a professionally managed Indian Multinational committed to total customer satisfaction and enhancing shareholder value.

L&T-ites shall be an innovative entrepreneurial and empowered team constantly creating value and attaining global benchmarks.

L&T shall foster a culture of caring trust and continuous learning while meeting expectations of employees, stakeholders and society.

Cynics claim that such vision statements are decorative wall pieces; remove the name and even the Chairmen and MDs would not be able to identify their company's vision statement. This does not appear to be the case at L&T.

'What makes L&T an outstanding and a unique organization?' was a question asked to more than 70 executives in Mumbai, Delhi, Chennai, Kolkata, Rourkela, Baroda and Dubai. These included A.M. Naik, a retired Deputy MD, six Professional Directors, VPs, GMs and a team of middle managers and young engineers at L&T. The reasons that make L&T unique and outstanding echo the vision statement:

- Pride in building India.
- Empowerment and delegation from day one.
- Experiment, innovate and learn from mistakes. Do not fear reprimand or chastisement.
- Hire only on merit.
- Transparency and honesty in all dealings.
- Adherence to the law, business through honest means.
- Ensuring space and respect to all individuals, irrespective of their years with L&T.
- Managed by professionals: no owner.
- Irrespective of loss or gain, customer promise and satisfaction must be delivered.

The creation of a strong brand requires a wider dissemination and endorsement of what the organization stands for. It is up to the organization to then walk the talk. At L&T, all the 40,000 plus employees seem to be doing so. It is an amazing unity of thought and action that helps to cement a strong brand.

Pride in building India

Despite being a hardcore B2B company, L&T touches millions of Indians each day. Whether you travel on a national highway through Panipat or visit the Bahai temple in Delhi, whether it is the many software techies whose office space happens to be in any of the IT parks in Hyderabad, Delhi, Mumbai or Bangalore or a farmer using an L&T starter for his water pump, when you use the longest flyover—built in record time—on the crowded A.J.C. Bose Road in Kolkata, or when you are a spectator at a cricket match at a world-class stadium constructed in record time or even whilst you cross the bridges on the scenic route of the Konkan Railways. In the last seven decades, L&T has touched the life of every Indian.

It has accepted challenges when competitors developed cold feet. The L&T stamp is ubiquitous. The brand is revered so much that people name unnamed roads—if they were constructed by L&T—as L&T Roads! (as seen in Rourkela, Coimbatore and many such places).

Empowerment and delegation from day one

A Director shared that since the last several years, in spite of the fact that he is the Chief, till date, not even a single supplier has come to meet him. Every thing is so well empowered and delegated that practically nothing of routine and function comes to him. Continuing, he shared that as his bosses never pushed anyone, he did not do so the same either. They never expected attention, and neither does he.

A VP with more than 30 years of experience with Engineering, Construction and Contracts division (ECC), shared that even when it was small in size, the company believed in delegation. Recalling the time when the construction of a Rs 50 million cement plant was taking place in South India in 1978, the leader of the project was only in the supervisory grade. In 1978, Rs 50 million accounted for nearly 10 per cent of the total revenue of ECC. To repose confidence at such junior levels, especially in construction jobs, where large sums of money are involved, would be beyond the belief of many. But L&T, through these practices, has demonstrated faith and trust in its human resource. He continued that such examples of delegation would appear unbelievable even in today's day and age, especially in a country like India.

Another Director recalled as to how in difficult and remote construction sites, through empowerment and delegation, L&T maintained high morale and cultivated family feelings in all employees. Trust, openness and frankness were the mantras which made even 15 hours a day of work a matter of joy and not curse. They remain passionately involved in the timely completion of highly complex projects. This spirit was eloquently expressed by a young manager: 'We may be stretched, but never stressed.'

A Director felt if you adopt intensive delegation and back it with quick response to suspicion, perhaps organizations can prevent youngsters from indulging in corrupt practices. Concentration of power breeds corruption. Through empowerment, even at the lowest level, one can achieve professional excellence and high levels of ethical standards. Every decision, irrespective of who makes it, appears to be logical and unbiased.

Experiment, innovate and learn from mistake: Do not fear reprimand or punishment

An engineer with only two years experience with L&T could not remember having being reprimanded by his bosses for committing mistakes. A Director recalled that when he was barely one-and-half years old in the company, he had a chance to handle the job of a textile mill in South. His boss was away on leave. L&T was highest in price. During discussions with the consultants of the textile mills, the young engineer suggested an alternative plan which was cheaper and also more profitable for L&T. The consultant asked him to accept the order on phone. But when the young engineer's boss learnt about the acceptance of the revised bid, he suggested that the contract be cancelled as he apprehended losses from it. This led to a piquant situation. Since the order was officially accepted, it went against L&T's policy to back out. L&T has always adhered to its commitments to customers irrespective of commercial consequences. Finally the GM prevailed upon the boss of the engineer and L&T went ahead with the project. Later, as it turned out, L&T made profits!

The same Director said that even when his technical knowledge was limited, he had opportunities to design several plants in power, fertilizer, petrochemicals and cement sectors. He was sent to Europe to learn machine foundation. L&T always nurtured people as if they were nurturing its own sons. Obsessed with quality, L&T never allowed short cuts. It never permitted shabby jobs even at the cost of delays and dismantling at very advanced stages of a project. No compromise on quality was the only dharma. In such situations profitability was secondary. Timely completion and finishing the construction jobs faster than the competitors have always been two great advantages of L&T.

Hire executives only on the basis of merit

The obsession with merit has been L&T's karma since inception. As mentioned by several other Directors who have worked for more than 40 years, both Holck-Larsen and Toubro were mainly looking for recruiting engineers and managers on merit. Having ensured merit, they never interfered in their day-to-day work. In fact they encouraged executives to come up with ideas for growth and then gave them full freedom to implement their plans.

Transparency and honesty in all its dealings

A Director proudly narrated what a stockist from North shared with him. This was regarding the honest behaviour of L&T's sales personnel. The stockist was surprised when the sales force refused to accept any support from him for their travel or entertainment expenses. This was contrary to the experiences of this stockist with the practices of sales personnel from many other well-known companies:

> We are very particular about these practices, whether it is a big sum of Rs 50,000 or a small bill for a party, L&T has been paranoid to ensure that its sales personnel do not get trapped in such temptations of day to day life.

A Director felt amused when a supplier to L&T, unaware that he is talking to the Director and the boss of L&T's division which was buying these components, kept on praising the honesty of L&T buyers (purchasing personnel). The supplier also shared several corrupt practices of the other Indian organizations. The Director concluded that whether it is selling or buying, L&T would always turn out to be a very honest and transparent organization.

An almost unbelievable incident was the narration of another Director: 'Big or small, I have never accepted any gifts from our stockist.' He recalled a 'Dealers Meet', where the wives of stockists were invited, which coincided with his birthday. Around afternoon, a group of stockists said their wives were very keen to present him a birthday gift. The group got very upset when the Director declined to accept the gift. This prompted a threat to boycott the evening function. He ultimately could make them appreciate the merit of his decision with simple but emphatic logic. He said: 'In our executive lives we would have many instances of receiving gifts. These acts of accepting gifts can be interpreted in several ways by our colleagues and lead to all kinds of wrong practices.' According to him, not accepting gifts of any kind has helped L&T-ites maintain a very honest and transparent face. He further argued that L&T has appointed its stockist on merit. Today, these practices have enabled L&T to withstand the attempts of MNCs to woo away L&T's dealers. Due to these policies and practices, its dealers are very loyal to L&T. In spite of being strong players in the globe, they have not been able to make a dent on the 50 per cent plus share of L&T's products.

Adherence to the provisions of law: Doing business through honest means

Like merit, the founders also adhered to the corporate value of doing business with honesty. They never encouraged any shortcuts by adapting corrupt means. Similar to sticking to the value of honesty, L&T has always believed to respect the law of the land. No matter what the provision of the law is, they believed that it is always good business to remain on the right side of the law.

Good corporate governance is good business—L&T has always believed in this. To comply with regulatory requirement is part of its DNA. Directors and employees claim that honesty is reflected through their practices. Thus, till they found the provision even for replacements, L&T kept on paying exercise to the government. One Director claimed that they do not need any code of conduct to be honest. It is ingrained.

Ensuring space and respect to all individuals, irrespective of their years of service with L&T

A set of engineers working at a construction site at Dubai felt that the space and respect provided in L&T is amazing. The fear or hesitation to experiment and innovate is non-existent. Commenting on the work culture of L&T, a Senior VP recalled his conversation with the GM of his division some 35 years ago. He had joined L&T in 1970, after working with a very well-known German MNC where he used to remain under stress due to his boss. While in L&T, he did not fear his boss, yet there was someone who was driving him. This someone was not the boss, but the freedom and empowerment L&T provided to him at such a low level. So, in the earlier company he was working for his boss, while in L&T he was working for himself. Thus it can be seen that his own standards were his motivators and his empowerment was his accountability.

Managed by professionals: Nobody is the owner

Like A.M. Naik, the Chairman and MD of L&T, all its seven directors are professionals. They began their career as graduate engineer trainees or accountants in a branch of the company and have put in more than 35–45 years of service with L&T. Each one could recall the freedom, empowerment, space and learning environment they enjoyed as young engineers. They were selected on merit, and then made their way up the corporate echelons on merit alone. When they joined, they had no relations in L&T. When they became directors of L&T, they had no godfathers anywhere, financial institutions or on the board of L&T, to favour them. Each had the humility to admit that when they joined L&T, they neither dreamt nor felt capable of ever becoming Director of L&T.

Reflecting on the true spirit of professional ownership, a Senior VP said that when Holck-Larsen died, the founder–director did not own more than 3,000 shares of L&T. Commenting further, he shared:

> L&T's fundamental strength is professional management. All Directors demonstrate tremendous professionalism. Merit alone has brought them

to this level. All the present Directors joined as graduate trainees, some 40 years back. Each has proved his merit. As they are there because of their merit, there is no politics between them and they are always working as a team. Their presence on board is an indication that any graduate engineer trainee of today can dream to become the Chairman of tomorrow!!

A.M. Naik, the Chairman and MD, reminisces:

I have asked myself what this company would have been if some one other than Holck-Larsen and Soren Toubro had set it up. The answer is simple. L&T would have been just another enterprise, shorn of those striking features and subtle nuances that set us apart. If L&T today is unique, it is because our founders were unique. If we are recognized as an organization of professionals, it is because they were professionals themselves. If we are respected for our values, it is because at the formative stages of the company, they put in place the systems we still adhere to.

Irrespective of loss or gain, customer promise and satisfaction must be delivered

L&T's business philosophy has always been to develop long-term business relations with its clients rather than think about a 'one time order'. 'Customer comes first' seems to have been its motto for long. The phenomenal growth of 29 per cent compounded growth rate between 1990 and 2008 in its sales and a long list of repeat customers of over 30 years plus testifies that L&T has been a customer caring and customer driven organization. Its impressive list of customers includes all the well-known companies in India. Some of them are: Tata Steel, Sterlite, GMR, GVK, National Highway Authority, Reliance Group, Atomic Energy Commission, Adani Group, and refineries like IOC, IPCL, HPCL, ONGC, GAIL and SAIL. The list would be very long.

'Commitments made, must be honoured' is like a religion to L&T. A director felt:

Even though, over the years, lot of systems and processes are in place to ensure profitable execution of the contracts, but till date customer satisfaction and delight is the primary consideration. There is no compromise on customer issues.

He reiterated dignity of staff and commitment made must be honoured.

The Enigmatic A.M. Naik: The Most Visible Face of Brand L&T CMD since 2004

At the 50th Convocation of XLRI, a leading management school of business of India, Mr Muthuraman, ex-MD of Tata Steel and Chairman of the Governing Council of XLRI, while introducing Mr Naik, who was the Chief Guest for the Convocation, mentioned that Mr Naik has worked for 80 hours every week since the last 20 years without taking any break. The only day he takes a break is on Sunday, the day when he still likes to play badminton, his favourite game.

Mr Naik joined L&T in 1962 and has remained steadfastly loyal to the company ever since. In 1992 he was nominated to be part of the Board. In 1996 he was appointed as the MD of the Board. In 2004 he was appointed the Chairman and MD of L&T which led to radical transformation of the Board. As felt by a Senior VP, Mr A.M. Naik's appointment could be considered as the most important turning point in the history of L&T. Through his aggressive, boisterous and earthy managerial style, Mr Naik is making an attempt to recast L&T-ites from mere good professional managers to entrepreneurial managers. He wants them to become bolder and take risks and to perform well within the systems and attain their targets. He feels that L&T as a group can accelerate its growth and become a global giant. For this he has set an ambition of achieving 30 per cent sales from global operations in the next three to five years. The project 'Lakshya' has been conceived to achieve very ambitious goal.

Since the 1980s L&T has remained in news for both its achievements and take over attempts by the likes of Ambani (Reliance Group) and Birlas (A.V. Birla Group). This situation of no major holdings by any family or promoters was a very attractive situation for any big business house to pick up the scrip from the market and gain control of the board room with the help of the financial institutions. For nearly 15 years, the professionals managing L&T remained preoccupied to prevent control shifting away from them to the families of the Ambanis and Birlas. But till the time the epoch making cement demerger was inked with the A.V. Birla group of companies in 2003, the professionals working with L&T were not too comfortable with the vulnerability and uncertainty about the board and its control. The move to de-merge the cement division to A.V. Birla group in 2003 and also the creation of 'L&T Employees Welfare Foundation' which by 2008 was holding around 13.13 per cent of the total holding of nearly 283,270,748 shares of L&T (face value Rs 2 per share) were two master strokes of Mr A.M. Naik which finally got rid of the uncertainty facing L&T and its employees. The creation and owning of 13.13 per cent shares by the Employees Welfare Foundation provided the 'ring fencing' from any takeovers.

Legendary Holck-Larsen Who Planted the Seed of Brand L&T

> Machinery must be there, buildings must be there but without the people, it's all nothing. People are our only real asset.
>
> —Holck-Larsen

This widely used quote by the company's people-centric co-founder crystallizes the pivotal role that employees play in L&T. Holck-Larsen was perhaps the only foreign industrialist to have spent more than 60 years in India. L&T is, and always was, an essentially Indian success story. Once, when asked what he would define as the single most important ingredient of his success as an industrialist in a developing country, Holck-Larsen replied: 'If you want to belong to a country which is becoming a nation, you have to keep the economy growing by creating jobs. And you can only do that by investing in tomorrow, and tomorrow is made by people.' So strongly are the company and its achievements identified with Indian aspirations that for years its theme line was: 'We make the things that make India proud.'

Holck-Larsen was a visionary in the true sense of the word. 'It is our ability to anticipate the future', he once said, 'and react accordingly that will determine our success'. L&T's distinctive place in the Indian industry, its spectacular record of achievements and its unique character are due, in great measure, to his inspirational leadership. The company's strong customer orientation and professionalism can also be traced to the values he instilled.

Arun Bharat Ram, then President of CII, said: 'There are many instances of creation of wealth. But Holck-Larsen created this for India!'

On 12 June 2008, the Government of India paid a richly deserved tribute to L&T's co-founder Henning Holck-Larsen. While releasing a commemorative stamp, A. Raja, the Union Minister of Communications and Information Technology said: 'Henning Holck-Larsen is an inspirational figure in India's corporate history. Men like him have played a pivotal role in the making of modern India. We are privileged to recognize his contribution by releasing a postage stamp in his honour.'

Corporate Social Responsibility: Company with a Human Face

L&T's Sustainability Report mentions:

> Decades before 'CSR' became a corporate buzzword, L&T and its people had been living their professional and social obligation. Climate change had not yet become a global concern, when we invested in cleaner and greener processes in our manufacturing facilities.

Recognizing the need to prioritize, L&T has identified three areas: mother and child's health; education at school level; and awareness programme for HIV/AIDS.

As the Director who champions CSR in the company put it: CSR is in our genes. We have day care centres at our construction sites. Acknowledging L&T's contribution, a primary schoolteacher in Powai said: 'L&T may be an engineering giant but I can state that it has made a world of difference to children.' With all the commendable assistance from L&T in smooth, excellent and efficient running of the school, it made her 'wonder whether L&T is in to material engineering or people engineering'.

Performance beyond Words

Paying tributes on ECC's 60th birthday (ECC accounts for more than 50 per cent of L&T sales), A.M. Naik stated:

> ... I have always described ECC as 'The Jewel' in the L&T's crown. The jewel has now acquired the sparkle of a diamond as it turns 60. Of all the activities of the conglomerate L&T, ECC's projects are the most visible to the public eye. Over these six decades, we have turned plots of land into landmarks. We have quenched thirst in arid districts of our country, linked places and people through bridges and highways. In every road that we built, we have set new milestones ...

Its employees boast that L&T never baulks or shies away from bold experiments. The bigger the challenge, the more spirited is the response. This is how it has been coming up with path-breaking achievements one after the other. Whereas its competitors were not trying the new routes, L&T accepted the challenges, its distinct trait being to learn from mistakes and own the responsibility for failures. All this has finally reflected in its business performance. In 1965, the sale of its construction division—popularly known as ECC—was less than Rs 10 million. It was smaller than the Hindustan Construction Company. But now the same division accounts for nearly 50 per cent of its L&T's sales of US$ 5 billion. Against its sales of Rs 120 billion, its competitors like Gammon are way behind: Gammon (Rs 36.5 billion) and Hindustan Construction Company Limited (Rs 33.73 billion).

A senior VP shared:

> Sometimes we feel that ECC cannot perform if there are no challenges in terms of quality and speed. We seem to have a healthy dissatisfaction

which keeps 30,000 plus staff going. Innovations are taking place in terms of execution time. Communication within the organization is fast and has improved a great deal.

Similar to the achievements of ECC, the other divisions too are proud of their achievements. Some of these are:

- India's biggest marine equipment—an oil and gas processing complex.
- One of the world's largest diesel hydro-treater project for a refinery.
- An 88 metre bridge on the Northern Railways' Jammu–Udhampur line.
- The world's largest coal gasifier manufactured by L&T and supplied to China.
- The world's largest Continuous Catalyst Regenerator (CCR) for a refinery.
- The world's largest ammonia converter for a fertilizer plant.
- India's widest range of switchgear.
- The Barbados stadium, venue of the 2007 World Cup final, built by L&T in less than two years.

Green L&T

L&T remains acutely conscious and concerned about environmental issues associated with its business. It leads the way in introducing plants and systems that incorporate environment-friendly technology. Given the nature of L&T's business, L&T's own operations have a minimal impact on the environment. Many of its business activities exhibit sensitivity towards environment. Some of these are:

- Facilitate the adoption of clean fuel technologies in refineries.
- Enable petrochemical projects and process plants to reduce emission levels.
- Proactively introduce environment-friendly technologies before they become a regulatory requirement.

- Facilitate the use of clean alternative energy sources through its association with the nuclear power programme.
- Focus on the challenging segment of super critical boilers and turbines that enhance operational efficiencies and minimize carbon emission.
- Venture into the construction of 'green buildings'.

Financial Performance: The Acid Test of a Strong Brand

> If you compare other companies' performance versus the Sensex, you won't even find five like mine. Secondly, many of these companies are very focused. Bharati Airtel in telecom, Tata Steel in steel, Reliance in petrochemicals and refineries and Reliance ADA group in energy and telecom. Not a single company in our sector in the whole world will enjoy a Market capitalization appreciation—now $27 billion—like us.
>
> —A.M. Naik

The acid test of a strong brand is its financial performance. Being a hard core engineering brand, L&T's profitability could never match the profits of IT services companies like TCS and Infosys. Against their profit after tax returns of 23–24 per cent on sales, for a company like L&T, these vary between 4 and 9 per cent (between 1990 and 2008). Further, the nature of business being engineering and construction, profitability is also linked to developments of economy—infrastructure projects; capital formation in terms of new factors; expansions and modernization. The flow of orders, cash and profits would not be even as that of near necessities and several other commodities like oil, petrol and steel. But, in spite of the constraints, L&T has maintained a financial performance which could be the envy of many organizations. Analysis reveals that L&T has maintained a cumulative annual growth rate (CAGR) of 24 per cent between 1990 and 2008 in its profits after tax (PAT). Similarly its CAGR for sales for the same period has been 20 per cent.

The de-merger of cement division unlocked the market value of share which was hovering between Rs 108 (in 1991) and Rs 183 (in 2003). By March 2003, L&T's market capitalization was around Rs 45.83 billion. By March 2004, i.e., within one year of the de-merger, it doubled to Rs 90.48 billion. By March 2007, i.e., within three years, it increased by four times to Rs 368.845 billion. And by October 2007, it was around Rs 894.68 billion, i.e., within seven months, the market capitalization doubled once again. On 1 November 2007, at a market price of Rs 4,550 per share, market capitalization peaked to Rs 1.28 lakh crore. This dream-run of L&T share was the vindication of A.M. Naik's hope and wish that with nearly 13 per cent of equity with the Employee Welfare Foundation, no raider would dare to take over the company. The 'ring fence' which appeared frail in 2003 had been fortified nearly 28 times in less than five years. This was truly a remarkable feat achieved by A.M. Naik and his team. This was corroborating with what a senior VP shared saying that the most important turning point in the history of L&T was the appointment of Naik as the Chairman and MD of L&T.

The Brand-Building Initiatives of L&T

The role of corporate communications

Unlike a large number of B2B organizations in India and abroad, L&T appears to have realized the payoffs from 'standardization' of communication efforts and use of its logo from very early days to become more visible in a cohesive manner to the outside world. No matter where they ply, Mumbai, Jamshedpur or Dubai, the buses of L&T have the same golden yellow colour. It is amazing that whereas companies making the chassis of buses have not cared to standardize on the colour of the fleet of buses they use for their employees, a hard core B2B company like L&T could think of reaping rich benefits of such easily available low cost alternatives for brand building. These golden yellow buses have become the most visible moving billboards of L&T throughout the country. Similarly all the signages of L&T have a golden yellow colour in the background, whether it is the boards or ribbons of ECC, at a construction site or a training centre of L&T Eutectic. L&T's corporate identity manual is a much thumbed road-map that guides employees, dealers and site personnel on how the logo and related brand assets should be rendered. Recognizing the importance of internal communications in brand building, it publishes several in-house magazines. Overseeing these activities is a team of 21 executives in its corporate communication department. The team, which is headed by a GM, covers A to Z of both internal and external communications. It even has its own team for copywriting and creative work. The corporate communication department is responsible for:

- Media relations
- Corporate branding
- Marketing communications
- Internal communications
- Recruitment advertising

Each activity is headed by senior managers with wide and deep experience in their area of expertise. Three days interaction with team members was convincing enough to state that corporate communication is not a side activity, but a very important support activity to make the entire L&T as a brand-driven organization.

Taglines of L&T over the years

A tagline reflects the dominant theme and the image a company wants to project to the external world. It is a very important part of the corporate brand. Some companies change it rather frequently and some companies, never. L&T from time to time has been announcing its changing spirit over the years. These have been:

- 'In Service Lies Success': It has survived the longest probably because its message is perennial and customer-oriented.

- 'Where Technology Moves with Time': With L&T's thrust on technology in the 1970s.
- 'People Our Prime Movers': This was there in the mid-1980s. People have always been pivotal to L&T's operations. It is an asset whose worth is indeterminable and its potential, infinite.
- 'We Make the Things that Make India Proud': A slogan that evocatively captures the strong nationalistic orientation of the company, and its engagement in sectors of crucial significance to India. Within the country, it remains one of the most well remembered of L&T's slogans and was quoted by the then Prime Minister of India Atal Behari Vajpayee when he inaugurated L&T's IT park, HITEC city in Hyderabad.
- 'It is All about Imagineering': This reflects L&T's increasing migration into knowledge-intensive businesses. The tagline was also directed to audience in new and emerging markets outside India.

Transforming L&T: To Brand-driven Business

Even though, L&T has put in substantial effort in brand building for both at corporate and product levels, but top management of L&T has cast an ambition to link everything of business around building a brand.

Reflecting the importance of brand building, Mr Naik had, for the first time (in the Annual Report of 2007–08), dedicated one full paragraph in his annual address to the shareholders of L&T. Highlighting the importance of building business around a strong brand, he shared:

> The L&T brand strikes a resonant patriotic chord across our domestic target groups. Consistent brand positioning has enabled us to establish a strong and memorable image of L&T as a 'Nation Builder'. Brand tracking and studies of various stakeholders affirm that public perception of L&T is on line with company's communication objectives. L&T's tagline—'Its all about Imagineering'—reflects the sharpening focus on knowledge-intensive business as the upper end of the technology spectrum.

Taking the direction from Mr Naik, the corporate communication department has developed a grand plan of four years for brand transformation. The key aspiration is to grow business revenues through brand leadership for all the 75 businesses of L&T. For several divisions, it may require raising some basic questions to bring more clarity on product and brand positioning, value propositions and identification of the dimensions for differentiation and uniqueness. Finally these should appear aligned with the overall corporate image of L&T.

Sustaining Endurance

A.M. Naik, in the same ceremony celebrating 70 years of L&T, proudly declared these 70 years as seven glorious decades of prosperity with honour and dignity. This chapter shared several reasons that helped make the L&T brand an enduring and inspirational industrial icon. The seed sown is such that the tree would remain evergreen.

This to my mind is the biggest challenge to Mr Naik and his team of directors for brand L&T.

6

Every brand has at its core a substance that gives it strength.
Your have to understand it before you can grow it.

—Scott Bedbury

6

Brand Infosys: Excellence in Never-ending Symphonic Marathon

We never dreamt about size, revenues and profits. Our dream right from day one was to build a corporation that was above all things, respected.

—Narayana Murthy (2005),
Chairman and Founder of Infosys

In a seminar on 'Creating Value Through Brands', I began my presentation by asking the participants whether they can name an Indian company which has given a 2,000 times return to its shareholders in a span of 13 years. The second question was to name a company where one share in 1993 became 64 shares by the end of March 2006. Sensing their uneasiness, I gave them a hint that this company was started in 1981 by a group of seven professionals with a total investment of Rs 10,000 (US$ 250) only. Seemingly, the hint was enough for a few in the audience to recognize the company as 'Infosys'. And by January 2008, Infosys market capitalization had reached US$ 20 billion (CMIE, Prowess Database, 2008).

Within a span of two years, its brand value increased from US$ 3.2 billion in 2005 to nearly US$ 8 billion by 2007–08. As compared to sales of US$ 100 billion of IBM, Infosys's is only US$ 4 billion plus (in 2008). Against IBM's 300,000 plus human resource, Infosys has only 100,000 plus (in 2008). So, Infosys has a long way to go. But then as compared to nearly 90 years of existence of IBM (which was started in 1911), Infosys is only 29 years (started in 1981) old. It took Infosys 23 years to achieve US$ 1 billion in sales, but it crossed US$ 2 billion in the next two years in 2006. By 2008, its sales had crossed US$ 4 billion. It is now galloping at a very high speed. Its CAGR between 1990 and 2008 works out at 60 per cent per annum which is way ahead of its main Indian competitors (TCS had a CAGR of 32 per cent per annum between 2005 and 2008 and Wipro had 29 per cent between 1990 and 2008). However, it is not the speed of Infosys's growth which is the subject matter of this chapter, but the 'symphonic marathon' it is running at breakneck speed. This is reflected in all its decisions: from managing its 570 plus customers, to the management of 3,500 vendors (Infosys 2008–09), to hiring and training its 100, 000 employees, to the management of hospitals, to the daily feeding of lunch to nearly 0.8 million schoolchildren. 'Compassionate capitalism', which Infosys wants to practice, has been possible due to sustained and superlative financial performance. The wealth created has been shared by all—shareholders, employees, promoters, financers, independent directors, and the society at large.

Symphony means a lilting music of a large opera comprising hundreds of musicians. It demands fine tuning at two levels. First is that of individual instruments. The second is when all the artists play together under the stewardship of the opera conductors. Infosys too is playing this lilting symphony ever since it began in 1981. All its decisions are finely tuned and continuously strengthening 'brand Infosys'. It is not by chance or luck that Narayana Murthy and Nandan Nilekani have become the most sought-after business personalities of mass media and many educational, economic and social forums. Scott Bedbury (2002: xiv) suggests that 'You have to earn trust and love by how you behave over time.' This too has been the mantra of Infosys from the day one. Reading its annual reports, sustainability reports, speeches and articles published globally, and corporate communications, one is awed by the depth, width and quality of thousands of decisions, which on one extreme covers the convenient timings for the housekeeping ladies from the local communities, to the creation of spectacular campuses which every President and Prime Minister from India and abroad wants to visit. Big or small, each decision reflects a very matured and deep thought, finally tuned to resonate with the brand Infosys.

The story of Infosys could be considered as the most fascinating story of a business corporation in post-independent India. The brand-building initiatives of Infosys appear to be echoing what James Gregory (2004: 3) suggests:

> A corporate brand is not a by-product. It is not an ad campaign, a logo, a spokesperson or a slogan. Rather, a corporate brand is the product of millions of experiences a company creates with employees, vendors, investors, reporters, communities, and customers and the emotional feelings these group develop as a result.

Chasing Respect: The Guiding Post for Brand Infosys

When the company began in 1981, the founders asked themselves a simple question: What are we going to chase? Are we going to chase revenue or profits or market cap or what? The answer was: No. They came up with a very simple concept: We will chase respect. We want to be the most respected company in the world (Narayan Murthy 2005). A long list of the awards is a testimony to that Infosys has outperformed its own aspirations. A glimpse of the glitter is shown in the following list.

List of awards

The honours board

- Among the 200 Most Respected Companies in the World—
  The Reputation Institute, 2007
- Among the TOP 10 Companies for Leaders—*Fortune Magazine*,
  Hewitt Associates and the RBL Group Survey, 2007
- Most Admired Company for the Sixth Time—*Asia Wall Street Journal*, 2008
- Most Respected Company—*Businessworld* Survey, *2006*
- Among the World's Top 3 IT Services Companies—
  Businessweek, 2004
- Best Outsourcing Partner—Waters Readers' Survey, 2007

- Best Company to Work for in India—*Business Today*, Mercer THS Survey, 2006
- Leader in Global IT Infrastructure Outsourcing—Forester, 2007
- NASSCOM—*India Today* Woman Corporate Award for Excellence in Gender Inclusitivity, 2007
- Global MAKE Award, 2003–05 and 2007
- Helen Keller Award for Diversity Hiring for Infosys BPO, 2006–07
- Balanced Scorecard Hall of Fame for Executing Strategy—Palladium Group, Inc., 2008.
- One of the World's Most Innovative Companies in APAC—*Business Week*, 2006
- CNBC-TV 18 Viewers Choice—New Age Employer of Choice Award, 2007
- One of the World's Most Respected Companies—*Financial Times* PWC Survey, 2004

Between 1993 and 2000, Infosys won 35 prestigious awards. But between 2001 and 2008, i.e., in the next seven years, it won 129 awards. The company now seems to be galloping in a geographical progression to win awards and recognition.

Creation of a Robust Brand

First thing first—The financial performance: Sounds unbelievable, but it is true. Infosys made profits from the year it began. In 1982 with a sales of Rs 1.2 million, it declared a profit of Rs 0.4 million. Even when chasing respect was the obsession, Narayana Murthy and his colleagues had recognized that minus financial performance, it would be difficult to create the organization of their dreams. Mere words would be wishful. The company's website quotes Narayana Murthy saying: 'The primary purpose of corporate leadership is to create wealth legally and ethically.'[1] He and his team have more than delivered on that. Table 6.1 is reflective of the superlative performance of Infosys.

Table 6.1   Profits and Employees over the Years

				Rs in Crore
Year	Sales	PAT	Employees	% PAT/Sales
1982	0.12	0.04	12	33
1996	89	21	1,172	23.5
2000	882	286	5,389	32.4
2004	4,853	1,244	25,634	25.6
2005	7,130	1,846	36,750	25.8
2006	9,521	2,458	52,715	25.8
2007	13,893	3,850	72,241	27.7
2008	16,692	4,659	91,187	27.9
2009	21,693	5,998	104,850	27.6
5 year CAGR	34		33	37

Source: *Annual Report*, Infosys (2008–09).

Recalling his journey with E. Raghavan and Mitu Jayashankar (in an interview when *The Economic Times* honoured him with the Lifetime Achievement Award on 27 October 2007), Narayana Murthy shared:

> In 1981, when I sat down with my colleagues, I said three things too them. One, this company would make profit from day one, because we will spend less than we earn. Two, we will declare dividends from year one and three, we will pay taxes from that dividend and put that back as equity. We were starting with equity of only Rs 10,000 and we wanted to go public in 10 years. So we had to grow the equity from Rs 10,000 to Rs 2 crore–3 crore. I am so happy and grateful that everyone agreed. (Raghavan and Jayashankar 2007)

The superlative financial performance made the promoters, along with many others, billionaires. As of 24 July 2009, when the share value of Infosys was Rs 2,003 per share, the family wealth of Narayana Murthy was Rs 57.2 billion (US$ 1.19 billion)[2] while they owned 5 per cent shares. The family wealth of Nandan Nilekani was Rs 39.85 billion (US$ 0.83 billion) and they owned 3.45 per cent shares. Gopalakrishnan's was Rs 38.38 billion (US$ 0.83 billion) and his family owned 3.35 per cent shares. K. Dinesh's family wealth was Rs 28.84 billion (US$ 0.6 billion) and they owned 2.51 per cent shares and Shibulal's was Rs 25.3 billion (US$ 0.5 billion) and his family owned 2.2 per cent shares. The wealth of the promoters rose from a mere sum of Rs 10,000 (in 1981) to Rs 180 billion (US$ 37.5 billion; see Table 6.2). This huge wealth creation, by maintaining 100 per cent honesty in a country like India would appear unbelievable. In the process they have also created 100,000 plus well-paying jobs, 2,000 plus dollar millionaires and Rs 20,000 plus millionaires (Infosys 2007–08). This creation of wealth is not only confined to its promoters, employees and shareholders, but has also been shared with independent directors. Since the last two years, each director has received more than Rs 5 million per year (approximately US$ 1 million). Very few companies in India have given so much to their independent directors as Infosys. Its governance principles also bar its own directors receiving any commission from the profits. This is in contrast to the commission earned by the company directors in several other well-known Indian companies.

The Corporate Governance: The Key Differentiator of Brand Infosys

The most outstanding aspect of 'brand Infosys' is its governance principles. These were put in place from day one to ensure a consistent, fair, honest and transparent performance all across its 46 offices and 100,000 employees (as in 2009). Looking at these, Mark Mobis, Manager, Franklin Templeton Emerging Market Funds, mentioned: 'Infosys's focus on Corporate Governance not only brought global visibility to the company, but also created pressure on other Indian firms to raise their governance standard' (Infosys 2005–06). Similarly, it prompted the distinguished Professor C.K. Prahalad from University of Michigan to state: 'The corporate model at Infosys has served as a powerful inspiration and motivator for entrepreneurial young professionals across the country. To him, this democratizing of entrepreneurship has been the legacy of Infosys' (Infosys 2005–06). Box 6.1 provides a glimpse of the governing principles.

Table 6.2 The Wealth of Promoters

Name of the Shareholder	[a] No. of Shares as in September 2008	% of Total Shares	[b] Rs in Crore Value of the Owners as on 24 July 2009 (Share Value Rs 2,003.65)
N.R. Narayana Murthy	3,179,672	0.56	637.09
Sudha N. Murthy	9,314,660	1.63	1,866.33
Akshata Murthy	8,106,412	1.42	1,624.24
Rohan Murthy	7,949,782	1.39	1,592.85
Total of the family	**28,550,526 (28.5 million)**	**5**	**5,720.52**
Nandan M. Nilekani	8,345,870	1.46	1,672.22
Rohini Nilekani	8,078,174	1.41	1,618.58
Jahnavi Nilekani	1,665,791	0.29	333.76
Nihar Nilekani	1,665,810	0.29	333.77
Total of the family	**19,755,645 (19.75 million)**	**3.45**	**3,958.33**
S. Gopalakrishnan	6,256,726	1.09	1,253.62
Sudha Gopalakrishnan	12,294,525	2.15	2,463.39
Meghana Gopalakrishnan	604,366	0.11	121.09
Total of the family	**19,155,617 (19.15 million)**	**3.35**	**3,838.11**

K. Dinesh	4,596,537	0.80	920.98
Asha Dinesh	7,047,482	1.23	1,412.06
Divya Dinesh	1,375,130	0.24	275.52
Deeksha Dinesh	1,375,130	0.24	275.52
Total of the family	**14,394,279 (14.4 million)**	**2.51**	**2,884.10**
S.D. Shibulal	2,469,711	0.43	494.84
Kumari Shibulal	2,811,044	0.49	563.23
Shruti Shibulal	3,671,924	0.64	735.72
Shreyas Shibulal	3,676,232	0.64	736.58
Total of the family	**12,628,911 (12.6 million)**	**2.2**	**2,530.39**

Sources: Prepared by the author. The data has been compiled from:

[a]: Infosys (2007–08).

[b]: Prowess Database, CMIE.

Box 6.1   The Governing Principles: A Glimpse

1. CEO would retire at the age of 60.
2. Zero tolerance towards integrity violators.
3. Always respect the law of the land where company has its offices.
4. Never make an attempt to manipulate the share prices.
5. Insisting on all the employees to maintain respect inspite of disagreement with their colleagues. 'You can be critical, but not discourteous.'
6. Ensuring a fair reward and ensuring low differentials between higher and lower levels.
7. Maintaining a variable portion of earning which could be linked to the performance of the company.
8. The Executive Directors would not to get any commission from the profits.
9. Ensuring the best use of the independent directors by selecting the best in their field and paying Directors through sitting fees and commission equivalent to what they would get in any leading MNCs.
10. Leaders must walk the talk.

Source: Prepared by the Author. The data has been compiled from annual reports of Infosys and interviews with Narayan Murthy.

Brand with a Conscience: The 'Brand Karma of Infosys'

Infosys did not wait for global development to show its concern for sustainability of the environment and society. The guiding spirit has been the following words of Nandan Nilekani:

> At Infosys, we believe that our future growth will only be viable and prosperous if we look at sustainability in all dimensions—environmental, social, political and economic. We are driven by a passion to be a good corporate citizen, and sustainability is at the core of operation.

Medinge Group, an international collective of brand experts who meet annually, chose Infosys Technologies Ltd as one of seven global companies to be in the first list of 'Top Brands With Conscience' (Kurian 2004).

Infosys's CSR policy focuses on five aspects of community development. It is organized around the acronym HEART: Healthcare, Education, Art and Culture, Rural Upliftment and Targeted Inclusive Growth. These include the Infosys Super Specialty Hospital at Pune, a pediatric hospital in Bhubaneshwar, an advanced pediatric facility at Wenlock Hospital at Mangalore, Community Eye Centre within the premises of the Shankar Netrayala Hospital in Bangalore, a pediatric hospital in Nilofur Hospital campus in Hyderabad and a general hospital for the tribal community in H.D. Kote, Karnataka. Besides the hospitals, Infosys has also created 15,000 libraries in schools across India since 2000. It has created 3.72 million sq feet of office space in Tier II cities across India in the year 2007–08.

It also supports 830,000 government schoolchildren for free mid-day meal initiative. Its concern about environment gets reflected through statements and information like:

- Eighty per cent of our employees based in India use public transport and company buses.
- Five per cent reduction in per capita electricity and fresh water consumption in fiscal year 2009.
- Thirty per cent green cover at all our development centres in India.
- Its annual reports are published on 100 per cent recycled paper.

The Success Mantra: Amazing Clarity and Focus

'Every company has to recognize its strategic resources and ensure their long term supply,' suggests Narayana Murthy. For Infosys, the three strategic resources are: human intellect, technology and process.

Reflecting the importance of human resource are the words of Narayana Murthy: 'Our Corporate assets walk out every evening. It is our duty to make sure that these assets return the next morning physically and mentally enthusiastic and energetic' (Infosys 2007–08). When Infosys began, it did not have even 100 employees in 1982. By 2008 it was employing more than 100,000 people. Since the last three years, it has recruited more than 20,000–25,000 people each year both from India and abroad. It receives 1 million applications and selects only 2.3 from them. One is appalled at the magnitude of the task of hiring the human resource. Recognizing the shortage of right talent and challenges of attracting and retaining the desired talent, Infosys has developed concepts like Campus Connect, Project Genesis, Industry Academia, Partnership in Project and InStep. Since 2005, Infosys has partnered with 1,256 colleges in India and countries like Malaysia. It has trained 4,200 teachers and 60,580 students.

Its *Sustainability Report* for 2007–08 shares that 33 per cent of its employees were women. Its employees are now from 70 nationalities. It spends as much as 964,205 person days of technical training for entry-level employees. But beyond the articulation of the critical resources is the recognition that speed, imagination and excellence in execution are time and context invariant to maintain competitiveness. In fact, speed in imagination is the most critical success factor.

Creating a Global Brand

'Today no one can deny that India is home to a world-class IT industry. Infosys, recognized globally as a leader technology solution company, has been the driving force behind this trend,' says Rajat Gupta, senior partner McKinsey and Co. (Infosys 2005–06).

In early 1998, Mr Narayana Murthy, had expressed an ambition that 'three to five years from now, when there is a $25 mn project, if the CIO were to ask he or her next in command whether the company had received the Infosys proposal, then I would feel we have arrived' (Ghoshal et al. 2001: 634).

Listing in NASDAQ, development of global delivery model, opening up of offices in 46 countries and with nearly 20 per cent of its human resources from places beyond India representing 70 nationalities, has made Infosys a truly global organization by 2008. But the master stroke of Infosys to become a globally-recognized organization was its association with Thomas L. Friedman. As shared by Aditya Jha, it was in the Infosys campus in Bangalore, that Friedman conceptualized the idea of famous book *The World is Flat*. It has made Infosys a widely-known global company.

Today 'Win in the flat world' has become the prominent tagline of all presentations and publications of Infosys. Infosys, instead of spending millions in global mass media, has been able to get substantial publicity without spending any money in mass media.

Managing Brand Infosys

In Infosys, managing brand is part of top management responsibility. Every quarter, the Chairman with his team of senior managers, review the brand performance with Aditya Jha, AVP, Corporate Marketing, Infosys. This is to ensure that brand Infosys is doing all that it is claiming. Walking the talk is what top management wants to ensure from everyone, irrespective of the level and location. Being a global organization, the task of alignment has become more challenging. For alignment, Infosys has identified four mechanisms. These are recruitment, orientation of new recruits, refresher work shops and leadership by example, i.e., walking the talk. Each mechanism ensures and reiterates the emphasis on following the Infosys values and its way of doing business.

Changing the brand perception over the years has been a constant endeavour of the Marketing Communication department of Infosys. But for these repositioning exercises Infosys does not spend in mass media. Instead, it spends more time on 'thought leadership', media relationship and management of events. The communication channels being followed are: online communications including the use of YouTube, public relations (PR) and relationship management with the corporate and financial analyst and management of flagship events in India and abroad. Dedicated teams of the marketing department are responsible to manage these four specific communication channels. These teams are global in nature and seek the expertise from whereever it is available within the organization.

Managing brand is managing business

To ensure that the brand-building efforts are working, Infosys firmly believes that business performance is directly linked with the strengthening of brand. So, besides direct communication efforts, each and every aspect of managing business is ultimately seen through the eyes of strengthening brand Infosys. Thus, Infosys treats investments in areas like project management, projects on energy conservation and similar such activities as brand investment. In order to gauge the impact of its brand-building initiatives, Infosys is amongst the few IT services organizations to calculate and track the worth of its brand. Basedon its own formula, the brand value of Infosys has moved up from US$ 3.2 billion in 2005 to US$ 7.9 billion in 2008 (Infosys 2007–08). This doubling of brand value in three years has not happened due to advertising and managing of events, but due to its firm belief that each and every activity of the organization should contribute to strengthening the brand and its value. As mentioned earlier, Infosys spends very little on marketing communication. Table 6.3 has the details of the last four years.

Table 6.3   Selling and Marketing Expenses (in Rs Crores)

Year	2005–06	2006–07	2007–08	2008–09
Sales	7,130	13,893	16,692	21,693
Expenses on brand building	46	69	55	62
Brand expenses sales (%)	0.65	0.49	0.32	0.28
Brand value (US$ million)	3,200	7,017	7,966	6,739

Source: Infosys (2006–07, 2007–08, 2008–09).

The Brand-driven Business

Perhaps no company other than Infosys from India comes near to what Dunn and Davis (2004) suggest for creating the brand-driven business. Citing examples of GE, Sony, Xerox, P&G and IBM and what they do, they write that these companies see brand not as a marketing communication icon, but as a critical business asset that must be protected and nurtured as much as other assets like people, equipment and capital. According to them, in these companies, brand has become integral to the overall strategic dialogue. It has become a critical filter for issues that might, on the surface, appear to be beyond the scope of brand's influence. Infosys has seemingly understood the idea very well.

What is the Never-ending Source of Energy and Endurance for Brand Infosys

While reading his speeches and interviews, perhaps the most favourite quote of Narayana Murthy appear to be 'The softest pillow is a clear conscience' and 'A good night's sleep is worth more than a billion dollars' (Narayana Murthy 2006). This conscience is continuously reinforced in its Vision, Mission and Values of Infosys (Infosys 2008). These are:

- **Vision of Infosys:** To be a globally respected corporation that provides best-of-breed business solutions, leveraging technology, delivered by best-in-class people.
- **Mission of Infosys:** To achieve objectives in an environment of fairness, honesty and courtesy towards customers, employees, vendors and society at large.
- **Values of Infosys:** To believe that the softest pillow is a clear conscience. The values that drives Infosys underscores their commitment to:

  o **Customer delight:** To surpass customer expectations consistently.
  o **Leadership by example:** To set standards in business and transactions and be an example for the industry and themselves.
  o **Integrity and transparency:** To be ethical, sincere and open in all their transactions.
  o **Fairness:** To be objective and transaction-oriented, and thereby earn trust and respect.
  o **Pursuit of excellence:** To strive relentlessly, constantly improve themselves, their teams, services and products to become the best.

Infosys Campuses: The Prime Icon of Brand Infosys

Around 1998 or so, Management Guru, late Sumantro Ghoshal and others wrote a case 'Infosys Technologies Limited Going Global'. They wrote:

> For an outsider, walking into Infosys is an unsettling, experience. Unsettling because Infosys was a combination of many elements which normally could not be combined. One could not but notice that there was something strangely different in the fabric of the company. Something very humane. The reception area led to a bridge over a little stream, running through a landscaped garden. The bridge led to canteen, a little kiosk which sold cool drinks, and snacks, and the basketball court .... (Ghoshal et al. 2001: 626)

What they experienced in 1998 is seemingly the case even now in 2009.

The Unsettling Experience

In September 2008, I left my hotel in Bangalore, around 8.30 a.m. to meet Aditya Jha, AVP, Corporate Marketing, Infosys in Bangalore. A journey of more than 90 minutes became unbearable even after 30 minutes. Finally the moment arrived when I was looking at the camera of the security personnel for my entry pass. The moment I hit a large central space—in the form of a square—I could get the glimpse of several buildings. While inquiring about Building No. 38 (Aditya's office), I could not keep my eyes away from a huge circular construction in front of the building at a distance from where I was standing. I was overwhelmed by the glow of the huge halo in front of the building. I started wondering whether the architect was Indian or foreigner. For a minute, I doubted whether I was in India or somewhere in West Europe or the USA. A flood of questions gushed through my mind which made me almost numb. Having stayed in Jamshedpur, the first steel city of India (created in 1907) by the most respected house of Tatas, for the last 32 years, I sensed a replication of the similar creation by Mr Narayana Murthy and his team of co-founders in Bangalore.

'What a creation in less than 30 years!' was a permanent thought in my mind. How could Narayana Murthy and his team do it? His background played in my mind. I recalled my MBA days at the Indian Institute of Management Ahmedabad in 1970. He was a Research Associate helping students like me to learn computers. None of my class fellows including me could sense the entrepreneurial genius of Narayana Murthy. With virtually no financial resources, how could they do it—besides the spectacular business performance, also create an immaculate campus with 50 high-rise buildings. Is it a campus in the garden or garden in the campus! With a virtual storm in my mind, I landed in Aditya's chamber.

After finishing discussions, Aditya accompanied me on a nearly 1 kilometre long walk cutting across the campus. Our final destination was Building No. 1, the first office of Mr Narayana Murthy. If he had not walked with me, I would have continued enjoying the most blissful walk of my life, but doing so, would have missed on the historical perspective of Infosys.

Building No. 1 houses a huge auditorium named after J.N. Tata. The plaque shown on him indicates 'Pioneer and Patriot'. The screen had a very prominently running display: 'Powered by Intellect, Driven by Values'. Aditya shared that it was in this hall that Thomas Friedman conceptualized the idea of his book *The World is Flat*. Next to this building, is a small, green ground meant to play golf. Aditya mentioned that it is very popular with Japanese clients of Infosys.

At every exit and entry point, I noticed dozens of umbrellas and cycles. Aditya mentioned that the whole campus is on a gradient. Cycles are very popular to move from one block to another. He also pointed out to the tree and tags of who is who of the world leaders. These included presidents, prime ministers, business leaders and statesmen.

Glimpses of the Iconic Leader—Narayana Murthy: Bold, Honest and Humble

Mr Narayana Murthy remains the most visible face of Infosys. Media has extensively covered his interviews and speeches given in India and abroad. These speeches are highly readable and quotable. Narayana Murthy identifies three defining moments of his life

(Roy 2005). One was when he was incarcerated in Bulgaria. Second one was when someone offered a million dollar to buy Infosys. The partners were keen to sell it off as US$ 1 million was a huge sum then. He prevailed upon them and persuaded not to sell the company off and break the partnership. As an alternative, in spite of having no money in his pocket, he offered to buy the shares of the partners.[3] At the end no one left and they continued to remain directors.

The third one was getting listed on NASDAQ–USA. As he shared, it was a small step for NASDAQ, but a giant leap for Infosys and the software industry.

In the mid-1990s, a very big global organization, which accounted for nearly 25 per cent plus business of Infosys, was pressurizing Infosys to reduce the rates to bring it at par with a competing Indian organization in IT services. The account was very critical for Infosys not only because of its share of its business, but also because of an association of several years. Recalling the incident, Mr Narayana Murthy said:

> We are grateful to GE; it helped us in learning an important lesson—that we had to de-risk our model. When GE decided to stop working with us (I am being very charitable), it formed 25% of our top line and 8% of our bottom-line. In May 1995, they registered all the vendors in different rooms in Taj Residency, Bangalore. We had a two day meeting, where they would discuss terms with each of our vendors in separate rooms and drive down prices.
>
> Finally, on the last evening, I took a decision that there was no way we could work on those terms. As I was coming back, Phaneesh Murthy was in the car with me. He had just become the Global Head of Sales. He was extremely upset and said: 'Mr. Murthy, you don't seem to be bothered about it.' I told him: 'I am as much concerned as anybody else but as the leader, I cannot show panic. But this is an extraordinary opportunity to start on a clean slate' (Raghavan and Jayashankar 2007).

Around April 2000, I was in Muscat (in Oman, part of the Gulf countries). I had a chance to meet an old friend from Jamshedpur—where I stay in India—who used to work with IBM in India. He left India around the late 1970s. Till the time I met him in Muscat, I had no idea of his whereabouts. By 2000, he was running his own computer services company with offices in Bangalore, India and Muscat, Oman. Even by 2000, my familiarity with IT companies and their performance was limited. They were not within my areas of research and interest. I had limited knowledge about some well-known companies from India like TCS, Wipro, HCL and Infosys. But what he mentioned about Infosys and Mr Narayana Murthy has been deeply entrenched in my mind forever. And what he said was that 'for the first time Mr Narayana Murthy has demonstrated to the entire business community in India, that one can become a billionaire by remaining honest even in a country like India'. And Mr Narayana Murthy—then and now, to my mind—is definitely has become the most honest face of India.

What is Brand Infosys is All About

If one were to sum up brand Infosys in few points then, perhaps, they may be listed as given below:

- Iconic leadership obsessed with the idea of compassionate capitalism.
- A brand with a human face and conscience.
- Outstanding financial performance.
- Unflinching integrity and total transparency and belief in the slogan: 'A clear conscience and a good night sleep is better than a billion dollar in banks'.
- Speed and quality in superb execution.

Long Live Infosys!

III

Brand Communications

Branding is endowing products and services with the power of a brand. Branding is all about creating the differences.

—Kotler and Keller

Strategy should evolve out of the mind of the market place, not in the antiseptic environment of an ivory tower.

—Al Ries, Positioning Guru

7

Managing Marketing Communications for B2B Markets

> Perhaps the most distinctive skill of professional marketer is their ability to create, maintain, enhance and protect brands. Branding has become a marketing priority.
>
> —Kotler and Keller (2006: 274)

The Importance of Communication

A widely-known view of brand pundits is that branding and brand management are way beyond mere awareness or creation of fancy advertisement, logos and taglines (Gregory 2004: 3). But without awareness and knowledge about their products and services, no marketer can sell anything. Contrast to B2C marketing, personal selling is the most important form of communication vehicle for the B2B markets (Sarin 1990). Researchers and practitioners share that 70–90 per cent of marketing communication is accounted by personal selling for B2B marketing (Sarin 1990). The balance would belong to non-personal elements for promotion and communication. The expenditure levels for majority of B2B marketers are so low (0.0001–1 per cent of sales), that the majority feels spending time on managing these elements is not worth the effort. Like many authors, my suggestion would be to spend wisely for long-term gains. The case of Shaktee Tools is a good example to share several issues which B2B marketers face to manage their small spends on communication and brand-building elements.

Many of the B2B marketers may find their experiences similar to Shaktee Tools. Besides sharing an illustrative case, I am also attempting to share some suggestions to mange the commonly-used communications tools like trade shows, publicity, public relations and media agent. Recognizing the increasing importance of websites in marketing communications, I have developed a separate chapter for effective management of the websites for B2B marketers.

Shaktee Tools: The Communication Issues

It was late in the evening. Everyone was keen to call it a day. These were seven to 10 senior executives of Shaktee Tools Limited (STL). They were waiting for the MD to approve the 'pull-outs' of the advertisement campaign for industrial tools. Industrial tools are needed by a very large number of industrial customers and freelance mechanics spread throughout the nation. The advertising agency had developed a three-series campaign. The executives wanted the final approval from the MD. In spite of the need for wider market reach, 'direct selling' by the sales people was the dominant strategy of STL. The MD of STL was never in favour of using the channel (distributors, dealers and retailers) to market industrial tools. His view was that selling of industrial tools, that his company was marketing, requires tremendous amount of personal selling efforts to even generate inquiries for submitting the quotations. And after submitting the quotation the sales team had to do a very close follow-up and frequent interactions with the members of buying centre—mainly users (technical personnel) and purchase department. Up till this point, i.e., before the use of print media for creating wider awareness, STL had mainly relied on product brochures, direct mailers and giveaways like diaries, expensive pens, annual calendars and some fanciful items for office use. On a sales of Rs 750 million (in 2008), STL's annual advertising and promotional spend was around Rs 2 million, i.e., 0.25 per cent of its sales. The company's total marketing expenses including the salary, travel expenses of sales personnel was Rs 40 million, i.e., around 5 per cent of sales. Personal selling, in this sense, was the most dominant vehicle for all communications needed for selling and brand building. The selling task included creating awareness, a generation of inquiries, providing information, inducing trials, closing the sales and order follow-up. The MD was happy that with this small spend of Rs 2 million; STL could achieve a sale of Rs 750 million by 2008. But as wider and deeper awareness could generate more demand and sales for the tools, the MD and his team were not sure whether annual sales of Rs 750 million was a good or poor performance. In other words, in spite of being in business for over 20 years, STL had no idea of the market size and potential of industrial tools in India. The GM, Marketing, for the industrial tools division was of the view that he could increase the sales by at least five times, i.e., Rs 3,750 million in two to three years' time. But for this, he needed to increase awareness and also market reach through distribution channel. For both, he felt that an advertising campaign in business journals like *Business Today, Business India, Business World* and in some dedicated trade journals would help. Against the wishes of his senior team members, the GM had been ruling out participation in trade fairs. His team members were keen to participate in at least 10 trade fairs in a year. The GM, Marketing, felt that trade fairs would be a waste of money for a product like industrial tools. He was willing to provide an additional Rs 3 million for promotional expenses but not for trade fairs. He wanted his team to come up with some less expensive and innovative ideas to create brand image and awareness. By providing the additional Rs 3 million, he felt that the sales should at least double to Rs 1,500 million in two yeas. His new proposal was as follows:

Promotional Elements	Amount (in Rs Million)
• Existing below the line promotional activities	2
• Print media in business and trade journals for a year	2
• Additional promotional expenses in low cost brand-building activities	1
	Rs 5 million

The MD was aware of the plans and views of the GM, Marketing, for industrial tools. He too was convinced that an increase in awareness and market reach would enable higher sales. In line with this, he had asked the GM, Marketing, to go ahead with the development of an advertising campaign for print media. The evening meeting was to approve the final campaign. While the campaign was being presented, the MD was feeling uneasy. Throughout the 60 minutes of the meeting, several thoughts crossed his mind. He quickly estimated that in the last 20 years, i.e., ever since he entered into the business of industrial tools, STL must have spend anywhere from Rs 250 to Rs 300 million. He wondered whether there could have been a more effective way to leverage the communication spend. He reckoned that after choosing the brand name (Shaktee Tools) and a corporate logo, his company had never raised any questions to judge the efficacy of what STL was doing. He was wondering whether there was a scope for harmonizing the brand-building efforts to create a strong brand. Playing back in his mind were the words of many experts which he heard at a brand summit he recently attended. Some of these were:

- A holistic marketing practice could help in building a strong brand.
- A strong brand can help buyers to shorten their decision process time. Has STL reached this stage?
- Every contact point—direct or indirect—affects the brand image of any organization. What people read, hear and see, experience, etc., affects the brand image and knowledge.
- More and more firms have come to the realization that their most valuable assets are the brand names associated with their products or services. Has STL any brand value and how can one know or calculate it?
- Branding is about creating difference. Has STL ever thought of creating a differential advantage to gain leadership?
- All money spent each year on manufacturing and marketing products should be treated as investment and not expenditure. The quality of investment is more critical rather than the quantity.

It was recognized that being a hardcore B2B company, the spend level would always remain very low. But should that mean that STL should not bother about effective use of the small spends on numbers of branding elements like giveaway, gifts, brochures, websites, sponsoring of events, seminars, trade shows, banner and print media? So before the approval of the advertising campaign, the MD of STL was keen that the GM, Marketing, take a stock of the past: what has been done and whether these activities have led to strengthening the brand? He wanted the GM to develop a holistic framework to evaluate the decisions on all the brand-building elements.

The question arising in the minds of the readers now would be: Why did I share the story of STL? It is to bring home the point that the situation of STL is neither unique nor unknown. Millions of B2B marketers, small or big, face the same situation; rather than being result-oriented, they have become victims of 'activity trap', i.e., doing things for the sake of doing. Even when small, all B2B marketers would always benefit by managing the branding elements. By managing their little rupees (on branding elements) well, the B2B marketers can manage and even reduce the expenses on personal selling. There is enough evidence which states that effective management of branding elements can bring down the cost or contact for personal selling. This in turn reduces the overall expenses on marketing.

Managing the Brand-building Elements

Reading the case of STL one can sense that STL would benefit by following a robust process of managing the branding elements. The process would include:

1. Brand audit.
2. Formulation of objectives for the communication programme.
3. Formulation of the budget for the communication programme.
4. Selection of the branding elements and roll-out plan.
5. Review of the programme and track studies.

Brand audit

Brand audit is a comprehensive examination of a brand involving activities to assess the health of the brand (Keller 2008: 76). For a large number of B2B marketers, the name of the firm itself is the brand, like STL's. This brand audit would almost be synonymous to 'corporate audit' as seen by the outsider. The outsiders here would essentially be the customers of STL. But if desired, the audit can include other stakeholders like suppliers, investors, prospective employees, and so on. The brand audit would entail digging deeper to tap perceptions and beliefs of customers towards STL. These can cover how STL is being perceived as compared to its competitors on parameters of quality, service, responsiveness, reliability, price and delivery performance. It should also include perception on STL's behaviour in terms of honesty, integrity and comfort of doing business with it. The analysis should provide information to strengthen and modify the communication programme. Frameworks of Young and Rubicam's power grid (Keller 2008: 417) gauging STL on brand stature and brand strength or Gregory's (2004: 11) suggestion to map STL on favourability and familiarity dimensions can also be used to analyse and to determine the present status of STL. Kevin Keller's 10-point brand score card (Keller 2008: 696) too could be a good framework to perform the brand audit. At the end, each B2B marketer should aim to develop its own framework for brand audit.

Formulation of goals and objectives for the communication programme

With the help of brand audit and the business objectives, the GM, Marketing, of STL and his team should identify the objectives and goals for the communication programme. Some of the commonly mentioned goals in the communication programme could be: changing the brand perception; strengthening and reinforcing the existing brand positioning; or increasing the awareness in some specific customer, industry and geographic segments. The objectives could also be to induce more trial for the products of

STL. It could be to enhance the market share for STL. As would be sensed, there should always be a multiplicity of objectives. It helps if they are few; to prune and select a few is a major challenge. At the end, these objectives should provide direction, clarity, challenges and excitement to develop the communication task. Lack of clarity can lead to a 'directionless activity trap' of a large number of B2B marketers. Identification of objectives and goals take time. A rush job can ruin the subsequent efforts.

Formulation of the budget for the communication programme

For majority of the B2B marketers the expenditure levels are very low. Due to this, there may not be any need to follow some rigorous and sophisticated process to develop budgets. Literature suggests (Webster 1984: 266–69) practice of four alternatives. My study conducted in the 1990s provides the comparison between the US and India as seen from Table 7.1.

Table 7.1   Budgeting Practices: India vs US

	Per Cent Responses	
Method	US	India
1. Per cent of anticipated sales	16	15.2
2. Objective and task	38	40.2
3. Affordable	33	29.5
4. Arbitrary	13	15.1

Source: Adapted from Patti and Blasko (Sarin 1990).

As evident from Table 7.1, the two most used practices are objective and task, and affordable method. It is my view that due to low expenditure level budget per se would not be a major issue. But using objective and task approach not only provides clarity but also objectivity in measuring the effectiveness of branding elements. Box 7.1 provides the reference of the ADVISOR projects. For researchers, these would be a good foundation to study the subject of B2B communications.

As a guideline, readers can also refer to Table 7.2 on communication expenditure levels of B2B marketers of India. Table 7A.1 provides the industry-wide expenditure level.

Box 7.1   Expenditure Levels for B2B Marketers: The ADVISOR Projects

ADVISOR (Advertising for Industrial Products: A Study of Operating Relationship) projects of Lillien and Little of MIT-USA (Lillien and Little 1976; also see Lillien 1976) were pioneering attempts to guide firms to manage the branding elements. Authors had attempted to provide the expenditure level of various branding elements. ADVISOR project had provided the data in form of percentages on three commonly-used terms. One was total marketing expenses to sales (M/S). The second was advertising (total spend on all the branding elements) as per cent to the marketing expenses (A/M) and the third was advertising (total spend on all the branding elements A/S) to sales. Tables 7.2 and 7A.1 have used the same ratios.

Selection of the branding elements and roll-out plans

Even in the IT era, personal selling would be the most important vehicle of communication. Personal selling is a broad term—it could include the CEOs to the lowest-level front-ranking sales executives. Besides the omnibus use of personal selling, a B2B marketer would need to select other branding elements. Refer to Box 7.2 for a brief description of major branding elements.

Box 7.2   The Brand-building Elements: A Brief Description

Building a brand requires use of the elements of marketing communication mix: The dominant elements are:

Advertising: Is a paid form of non-personal communication about an organization, product, service or idea by an identified sponsor.

Personal selling: Any paid form of personal presentation of goods and services. Face-to-face communication between the sender and receiver.

Publicity: A non-personal, indirectly paid presentation of an organization, service or product is termed as publicity.

Sales promotion: A short-term inducement of value offered to arouse interest in buying a product or service.

Public relations: It is an important activity which is done by all from CEO to the employees of the Public Relations (PR) department.

Websites and Internet: The use of electronic medium.

The selection should be linked with the effectiveness of these elements for different communication tasks. These tasks should cover activities like awareness creation, enquiry generation, product evaluation, information about company and products and the like. Table 7.3 provides a glimpse of branding elements.

Table 7.2 Communication Expenditure Levels of B2B Marketers: Range, Mean and Median

	1990[a]	2007[b]			
	Sample Size = 50	Sample Size = 1,434			
	VHS (%)	HS (%)	MS (%)	LS (%)	Range (%)
1. Marketing sales (M/S) (%)					
Mean:	5.6	1.7	1.3	1.6	
Median:	4	1.5	1.1	0.9	
Range:	0.03–21	1–2.4	0.5–3	0.4–5	0.4–6
2. Advertising marketing (A/M) (%)					
Mean:	2.2	43	27	4	27.75
Median:	18	37	22	3	
Range:	22–46	30–60	6–62	0.4–10	0.4–60
3. Advertising sales (A/S) (%)					
Mean:	1.5	0.67	0.24	0.05	
Median:	1.8	0.69	0.25	0.06	0.6
Range:	1.1–2.5	0.57–0.81	0.02–0.5	0.01	0.01–2.5

Sources: [a]: Sarin (1990).
[b]: Based on data available from Prowess Database, CMIE.

Notes: VHS: Very high spenders
HS: High spender
MS: Moderate spender
LS: Low spender

Table 7.3   The Communication Mix Elements

Advertising	Sales Promotion	Public Relations	Personal Selling	Direct Marketing
• Print and broadcast ads	• Premiums and gifts	• Press kits	• Sales presentations	• Catalogues
• Packaging outer	• Sampling	• Speeches	• Sales meetings	• Mailings
• Packaging inserts	• Fairs and trade shows	• Seminars	• Fairs and trade shows	• Fax mail
• Brochures and booklets	• Exhibits	• Annual reports		• E-mail
• Posters and leaflets	• Demonstrations	• Charitable donations		• Voice mail
• Directories	• Rebates	• Sponsorships		
• Reprints of ads	• Entertainment	• Publications		
• Billboards	• Trade-in allowances	• Community relations		
• Display signs	• Continuity programmes	• Lobbying		
• Point-of-purchase displays	• Tie-ins	• Identity media		
• Audio-visual material		• Company magazine		
• Symbols and logos		• Events		
• Videotapes				

Source: Adopted from Kotler (2003: 564).

The major challenge would be to achieve an integrated approach for a cohesive impact.

The roll-out plan

The roll-out plan would require a development of a calendar of activities. This should indicate as to when execution of different brand elements would be needed. There could be some regular activities spread over the entire year. These could include participation in trade fairs, organization of seminars, mechanics meet and visits of the customers to the plant. The other set of activities could be like distribution of diaries, calendars and other New Year gifts. It should reflect good combination of both below the line and top of the line activities.

Below the line activities are sufficient to build strong B2B brands: A view from the expert

Jasubhai Group[1] has over 30 years of experience for verticals in B2B markets. Sarita has been CEO for Jasubhai for several years.

Sarita feels that B2B marketers have greatly underrated the power of marketing communications to create B2B brands. The marketers have not made attempts to align their communications with what customers need and wants. It is her view that if you cannot engage your customers in your communications, you would lose them.

Sarita is canvassing for a paradigm shift in organizing seminars in which instead of marketers talking to the customers—customers talk about the brand. This is what she did for 'Structura' brand, the tubes division of Tata Steel. Between 15 August 2007 and 26 January 2008, it organized contest amongst the architects. Four hundred designers participated in the contest called 'Notions of a Nation', India. Teams of architects and engineers participated in the contest to develop new shapes and more end uses using the hollow sections. So instead of a dull monologue of marketers to the invited customers, we try to create participative and exciting seminars. B2B marketer should also learn to conduct experience-based seminars. Sarita feels that these are more effective. Through this, the customers learn from other customers and influencers like architects and designers.

Sarita suggests that for B2B markets, one need not advertise in the main stream media. 'Below the line' activities are sufficient to build strong B2B brands. She also says:

> But B2B marketers have yet to learn how to use the available 'below the line' options in a manner that contributes in brand building. Majority are following blindly, the practice of giveaways like calendars, diaries and alike. These are wastes. They can be more creative in their giveaways. B2B marketers need to learn to communicate in aesthetic manner. This can be simplified.

She also feels that B2B marketers need to respect the fact that their customers are taking business decisions. Marketing communications should help them to take better business decision. So far, according to Sarita, only 5 per cent of B2B marketers have realized the potential of online communication. This would become the most powerful tool for B2B communication.

The nuts and bolts of communication elements: Some ideas from the field

Though very difficult to generalize, based on my interactions with a large number of B2B marketers, an illustrative list of some top of the line (TOL) and below the line (BTL) promotions, including tentative expenditure levels, is shown in Table 7A.2.

Publicity, public relations and media relations

Personal selling accounts for nearly 70–90 per cent of the sales and marketing activities for majority of B2B marketers. Besides personal selling, a very important dimension of B2B marketer is PR and relationship management. The CEO and top management team of any organization, large, medium or small, has to be involved in relationship building with all the stakeholders. The amount of time spent in relationship activities, though never accounted for in annual reports and profit and loss (P&L) statements, should be considered as the most important brand-building activity.

Unlike large organizations like Tata Steel, L&T, AV Birla Group, Airtel, Reliance Industries and many more, the majority of B2B marketers are essentially a one-man show. They try to maintain a relationship with the stakeholders like bankers, investors, suppliers and customers with prospective employees. Providing quality time for PR and relationship management should be seen as brand-building activities. The B2B marketers should always make an attempt to leverage their relationship management for brand building.

A one-page ad in *India Today* cost Rs 0.3 to 0.4 million in 2009. A one-page ad in *Business Today* cost around Rs 0.19 million in 2009. Almost similar are the rates for other popular business magazines like *Business World*, *Business Today* (see http://ads. economist.com; accessed on 25 August 2009). A 30-second spot on popular TV channel may cost as high as Rs 0.2 to 0.3 million per exposure. Similarly, a half-page in *The Economist* may cost Rs 1.7 million and an ad at the back and front cover of the same may cost as high as Rs 8.7 million per insertion. In short, mass media is very expensive and beyond the means of many. For well-known companies, their CEOs are sought after by media. In India, not all CEOs and companies have achieved the iconic status and visibility of Ratan Tata, Narayana Murthy, Sunil Mittal, Mukesh Ambani, Rahul Bajaj or Kumar Mangalam Birla of AV Birla Group. Media seeks them for their views on government policies and economic developments. They have also become spokespersons for their industries. So, if it is auto industry, media's first choice could be Ratan Tata, Rahul Bajaj or the Munjals of Hero Honda. If it is telephones and mobile phones, Sunil Mittal today turns out to be the first choice. And any development in the IT sector, the first choice is Narayana Murthy of Infosys or Azim Premji of Wipro. If it is construction and engineering, it could be A.M. Naik of L&T. This has happened because of the management of media by their corporate communication departments. But, for a large majority of B2B marketers, this may be beyond their resources. Could there be a way whereby these SMEs also could get media coverage without spending substantial amount?

Here is list of activities which may help SMEs to get coverage in media:

- Try to become an active member of the association. Aim to become an official of the association at the local to national level. These could be like plastic traders association to sub-committees of CII.
- Identify the schools and colleges who could be the source of talent (Human Resource).
- Do not miss on supporting small collaterals like sponsoring bags, T-shirts, caps or even water bottles.
- Try to become an active member of some social clubs like Rotary or others and get involved in social activities for which you could have had a passionate and honest involvement. This will help you to get into local and regional level media.
- Identify some activities of town where you can have opportunities to sponsor some events and activities.
- Identify some useful gift items, which you can distribute locally on a regular basis.
- Try to become a spokesperson to the cause of local industry association, where you get a chance to interact with the government officials and also get an opportunity for media coverage.
- Sponsor some activities which could help you to build relationship with the investors' community.

Some of you may argue that you are neither PR nor a media savvy person. You may also feel that, all the PR and relationship management activities are superfluous and have no impact on the business. A few may argue that to begin with you are essentially a shy person and would like to maintain a low profile. Another group can argue that all the relationship management activities are a waste of time with no tangible contribution to your business. Some others may cite the examples of CEOs belonging to large (both family-managed and professional organizations) who have maintained a very low profile and yet have been very successful. That is true. It takes all kinds of people and possibilities to make this world. But what is being suggested is that there are variety of alternatives to choose from, to build the brand of one's organization. It is your choice to involve in those activities which suits your temperament and personality. One must remember, one has to be genuine and sincere in his or her approach. If you do not have 'relationship cultivation and management' in your personality, you should opt for several other brand-building elements.

PR: The two extremes—What would you pick?

Case 1: High on visibility, low on credibility: He never misses an opportunity to come into public limelight. He has been doing it for last 35 years, i.e., ever since he became an entrepreneur. His major business domain is B2B marketing. The product line includes engineering presses and fabrication of chemical plants. He always entertains his guests customers, bankers, technology partners, government officials and alike in five star hotels where all his conferences and seminars are organized. His giveaways are always useful and reflect a lot of taste and exclusivity. His brochures, letter heads, office furniture appear attractive and aesthetic in nature. In short, whatever is connected with the outer world is managed very thoughtfully and tastefully. He spends nearly four hours every day on PR and relationship activities. This he has been doing since the last 35 years.

He is an ace salesman and so is his team. Thus, when it comes to order-taking, he and his team come out to be the winners. But after that, the orders are never executed in time. There are delays and penalties. But so far he has been able to 'manage' it. But beyond his immediate customers and suppliers, and inspite of all the PR and publicity, his organization is a non-entity. He is an unknown entrepreneur. Media has never sought him. Prospective employees have never sought his organization as it is not known in the campuses of engineering colleges. Each time he hires someone, he has to explain what his company does, about its products, about its performance.

Thiry-five years have passed and yet nothing of substance seems to be in place.

Case 2: A low profile group: Low on visibility, high on credibility: In all, the group has five medium size organizations dealing in auto components. The combined sale of the group was around Rs 20,000 million (in 2008). All five firms are public-listed companies. The promoters own majority of shares. In all, the group may be employing more than 3,000 workers and approximately 300 managers and executives. Most of them would be engineers (graduate or diploma-holders). The present team of top management always maintains a low profile. But by virtue of their performance and size, the MDs have been on the managing committees of the regional chapters of associations relevant to auto component industries.

The group has maintained steady growth in sales and profits. The group also enjoys a good reputation with its customers. It has never believed in indulging in any PR activity. They have seldom sponsored any major national event. The group has never come out with any giveaways. Its management team has never appeared in any mass media.

The group has set up schools and training institutes in and around their factories. It has also remained on the 'right side' of the law. It has never failed to abide by their financial commitments, be it salary of employees, statutory dues of government or payment of its suppliers.

Will it pay if the group makes an attempt to increase their visibility?

Trade shows and exhibitions

Trade shows and exhibitions are considered to be very important communication platforms for the B2B marketers. In the year 2007–08, India had around 2,000 trade fairs and exhibitions. For a large number of companies producing industrial products, participation in these trade shows and exhibitions has almost become mandatory (see Table 7A.3). Elgi Equipments, a Rs 5,000 million company manufacturing air compressors, maintains a list of nearly 200 fairs that it can participate in India. Elgi participates in 30 fairs each year. Over last 10 years; it has also been participating in the Hanover fair. It feels that participation in the German fair has helped Elgi a great deal in increasing its awareness amongst the global customers. Like Elgi, L&T, the engineering giant from India has been participating in trade fairs over the last 30 years both within and outside India. For 2008–09, it was planning to participate in nearly 25 exhibitions in India. Tata Steel participates in nearly 15 trade fairs. Out of these, 10 fairs may be small and the remaining five very big fairs. These fairs could cost anywhere from Rs 3.5–10 million per fair. As per website report Buyer.com (2007) the size of the Indian advertising industry was Rs 180,000 million (US$ 3.75 billion) in 2007. According to them B2B marketers accounted for Rs 7,500 million (US$ 156 million), i.e., around 4 per cent of the total spend. The breakup for this Rs 7,500 million of B2B marketers is as follows:

- Publishing: Rs 2,810 million (US$ 58 million)—37 per cent
- Exhibitions and trade shows: Rs 4,210 million (US$ 87 million)—56 per cent
- Online advertisement: Rs 480 million (US$ 10 million)—6.5 per cent

Over the years, the Indian companies have increased their participation in the international fairs. Like personal selling websites and product catalogues, trade fairs and exhibitions would remain a permanent feature of the branding activities of a large number of B2B marketers. The challenge is to keep on increasing their effectiveness without increasing the spends.

Feedback and track studies

Track studies are conducted to check the success of communication programmes, whereas a brand audit is done on a non-recurring basis to modify the perceptions. Track studies are conducted on a regular basis to monitor the effectiveness of the branding programme.

In case of B2B marketing where ad expenses are very low, marketers also feel that track studies cost more than the actual cost of communication programme. So the majority of B2B marketers try to measure the effectiveness through tangible gains like premium on brands, brand loyalty, market share gain and growth in sales. The logic is simple that if business is improving, the communication campaign is also working. Thus, depending on the situation, B2B marketers may decide to conduct track studies on a regular basis. Keller's (2008: 347) book has some very useful suggestions. Track studies are normally conducted by professional organization. Small and medium size organizations may do these studies on their own. But from time to time, outsider's assessment would provide more objective assurance.

Summing Up

Holistic brand management: The ultimate challenge of branding

Authors in the area of brand management suggest following the holistic brand management approach (Kotler and Pfoertsch 2006: 16). The integrated branding approach requires a well orchestrated use of all brand-building elements. These brand-building elements, even for B2B marketers can run into hundreds and hundreds of options. Table 7.3 provides a glimpse of these elements. Coupled with the multiplicity of the options is the reality of low spends on branding activities of B2B marketers. Thus, in India, HUL, on a sales turn over of Rs 132,000 million (in 2007–08), had Rs 13,000 million as its advertising expense. The advertising to sales work out to be an A/S ratio of 9.65 per cent. For the same year, a hardcore B2B company like L&T, on a sale of Rs 180,000 million, had spent only Rs 500 million in advertising. For L&T, the A/S works out to be 0.27 per cent. Similarly Infosys, the IT service provider from India, on a sale of Rs 157,000 million, had spent around Rs 500 million as advertising expenses. This works out to be 0.31 per cent of A/S.

Similar differences exist amongst the global giants like P&G and GE. Thus, P&G, the largest spender on advertising, had spent nearly US$ 8.52 billion on its sales of US$ 57 billion (in 2007). This works out to A/S of 14 per cent. Against this, for GE, a predominantly B2B company, the advertising expenditure was around US$ 1 billion on sales of US$ 157 billions (in 2007). This would be around 0.6 per cent of A/S. (See Tables 7.4 and 7.5 for handy comparisons.) This finally leads to the conclusion that brands and branding have no role for the B2B markets. Because of this low expenditure, B2B marketers question the wisdom of spending executive time to ensure an integrated approach: 'Is the money spend worth the efforts?'

Table 7.4   Global Companies: Sales and Advertising Expenses

| Name of the Co. | US$ Billion (2007) | | % |
	Sales[c]	Advt. Expenses[a,b]	A/S
IBM[b]	91	0.6	0.65
P&G[a]	68	8	11.7
GE[a]	157	1	0.63
	P&G expenses are 13 times more than IBM and 8 times more than GE		

Sources: [a]22nd Annual Report: Global Marketers, *Advertising Age*, 8 December 2008. Available online at http://adage.com/globalmarketers08/#global_100 (accessed around January 2009).
[b]http://adage.com/marketertrees08/index.php?marketer=227#225.
[c]Fortune global 500 2007; available online at http://money.cnn.com/magazines/fortune/global500/2007/full_list/index.html.

Table 7.5   Indian Companies: Sales and Advertising Expenses

| Name of the Co. | US$ Million (2007) | | % |
	Sales	Advt. Expenses	A/S
HUL	2,700	200	9.65
L&T	3,700	10	0.27
Infosys	3,300	10	0.31
	HUL expenses are 28 times more than L&T and Infosys		

Source: CMIE, Prowess Database; Prowess is a database of large and medium Indian firms. It contains detailed information on over 23,000 firms.

Branding Payoffs: Accident or through Design

What ultimately happens is worded well by Hague and Jackson (1994: xii): 'Where industrial companies are already benefiting from branding, it is often by accident than design. However with little extra effort and cost, the effect would be much improved. With better branding will come improved business, improved loyalty, and greater profitability.'

Low spend should not be construed as no brand. So irrespective of what you spend, Rs 10,000 or Rs 100 million, every marketer could benefit by spending wisely. What is needed is deep thinking to become more innovative and imaginative.

Annexure

Table 7A.1 Expenditure on Marketing Communication as % to Sales (A/S)

Very High Spenders	% A/S	High Spenders	% A/S	Medium Spenders	% A/S	Low Spenders	% A/S
Furniture (11)*	2.52	Plain paper (41)*	0.81	Construction machinery (16)*	0.48	Compressors (17)*	0.10
Refrigerators (6)	1.63	Conveyer belts (7)	0.79	Ceiling fans (3)	0.45	Grinding wheel and abrasives (5)	0.09
Air conditioners (15)	1.56	Material handling equipment (25)	0.67	Gears (14)	0.30	Logistic services (35)	0.08
Packaging material (77)	1.44	Machine tools (73)	0.66	Electrical switchgear (34)	0.28	Aluminium products (44)	0.07
Floor tiles (21)	1.35	Auto component manufacturing (205)	0.61	Dairy equipment plants (3)	0.27	Industrial chemicals (35)	0.06
Bathroom fittings (4)	1.36	Cement (63)	0.58	Medical equipment (5)	0.27	Electrical transformers (28)	0.06
Paints (84)	1.29	Furnishing fabrics (8)	0.57	Courier services (7)	0.25	Welding equipment (14)	0.05

Industry (players)	Value
Audio-visual equipment (18)	1.25
IT industry (59)	1.14
Electrical appliances (52)	1.15
Cement plant machinery (5)	0.24
Earth moving machinery (13)	0.23
Pumps (34)	0.20
Electrical power cables (42)	0.18
Elevators (3)	0.18
Carpets (9)	0.17
Castings (91)	0.10
Copper wires (3)	0.02
Welding electrode (10)	0.05
Lubricating oil (21)	0.05
Petroleum products (50)	0.03
Transporters and bulk carriers (26)	0.03
Forgings (32)	0.03
Wire rods (11)	0.03
Mining equipment (8)	0.03
Bearings (16)	0.01
Steel wire rods (23)	0.01
Packaging plant machinery (3)	0.01
Diesel engines (2)	–
Electrical fittings (3)	–

Summary statistics:

	Total	Mean	Median	Range
(347)	1.4	1.5	1.8	1.1–0.5
(422)	0.6	0.67	0.69	0.5–0.8
(282)	0.2	0.24	0.25	0.02–0.5
(383)	0.04	0.05	0.06	0.01–0.1

Source: CMIE: Prowess Database 2007; Prowess is a database of large and medium Indian firms. It contains detailed information on over 23,000 firms.

Note: *signifies the number of players.

Table 7A.2 Illustrative List of Expenses on Promotional Elements

Top of the Line (TOL) Promotions Examples and Tentative Expenses		Below the Line (BTL) Promotions Examples and Tentative Examples	
Activity	Expenses	Activity	Expenses
1. Participation in trade—shows and exhibitions		10. Small collateral like T-shirts, caps, badges, name tags	Tentative expenses Rs 25–200 per item
a. Outside India	Rs 5–10 million per show		
b. Within India	Rs 10,000–5 million per show		
2. Development of a world-class product brochure	Rs 100–250 per brochure	11. Sponsoring of tea and lunch in industry seminars	Rs 50,000–0.2 million per event
3. Road shows and event sponsoring for promotions	Rs 0.1–1 million per show	12. Special gifts to the delegates attending trade shows, seminars, workshops	Rs 500–5,000 per gift
4. Hoardings in towns, cities and metros	Rs 0.1–0.5 million per year per hoarding	13. Stockiest meet outside or within India	Rs 15–20 million per meet
5. Development of websites	Rs 1,000–2,000 per page	14. Training camps for electricians, mechanics, etc.	Rs 250–1,000 per mechanics
6. Exclusive products display windows	Rs 25,000 per window	15. Free gifts (there could be some very expensive gifts for very special people)	Rs 50–500 per gift
7. Space in retail outlets	Rs 25,000 per window	16. Free health check-up camps in rural markets	Rs 50–200 per person
8. Point of purchase material at shops and offices of stockiest	Rs 3,000–5,000 per stockiest		
9. Advertisement in select trade journals	Rs 5 million per year		

Source: Developed by the author.

Table 7A.3   Indian and International Trade Shows Held in India in 2007 and 2008

S. No.	Industry	No. of Trade Shows
1.	Agriculture	43
2.	Apparel and clothing	78
3.	Architecture and interior designing	106
4.	Auto and automobile	42
5.	Aviation	16
6.	Ayurvedic and herbal	12
7.	Beauty and cosmetics	53
8.	Books	8
9.	Chemicals and dyes	23
10.	Computer and IT	59
11.	Construction	101
12.	Defence	12
13.	Education	81
14.	Electronics and electrical	100
15.	Environment	23
16.	Finance and investment	57
17.	Fire fighting and safety equipment	30
18.	Food and beverage	71
19.	Furniture and furnishings	77
20.	Gems and jewellery	68
21.	Gifts and handicrafts	47
22.	Glass and glassware	7
23.	Health and fitness	45
24.	Household consumer goods	36
25.	Jobs and career	8
26.	Leather	7
27.	Logistics	20
28.	Media and advertising	54
29.	Medical equipment	16
30.	Metals and minerals	13
31.	Packaging	42
32.	Pharmaceuticals	25
33.	Photography	17
34.	Plant and machinery	84
35.	Plastics	17
36.	Power and energy	43
37.	Printing and publishing	26
38.	Pulp and paper	3
39.	Railways	9
40.	Real estate and housing	52

(Table 7A.3 Continued)

(*Table 7A.3 Continued*)

S. No.	Industry	No. of Trade Shows
41.	Rubber and rubber products	8
42.	Sanitary and hygiene	5
43.	Science and technology	48
44.	Shipping	13
45.	Sports goods and equipment	8
46.	Stationary and office supplies	24
47.	Telecommunications	31
48.	Textiles and garments	51
49.	Tools and testing equipment	64
50.	Travel and tourism	48
	Total	1,931

Source: http://www.indobase.com/events/category-type/trade-shows.php

The information technology, Internet and e-mail, have practically eliminated the physical costs of communications.

—*Peter Drucker*

The Internet is becoming the town square for the Global village of tomorrow.

—*Bill Gates*

Internet is the Viagra of big business.

—*Jack Welch*

8

Websites and B2B Brands: A Low-cost Goldmine Lying Unexplored

The Webbed World

The first use of the Internet was done by the US government in 1958. The commercial use of the Internet began in 1989 (formation of the World Wide Web). As per Net craft[1] (a research group providing website survey services), by 2009, there were around 240 million websites.

With millions of websites around, we are living in 'webbed' world. From professor to punter, from a non-profit organization to a giant commercial organization, all are keen that people visit their websites. As per Wikipedia,[2] everyday, and this was in the year 2006, the search engine 'Google' received 400 million queries. It handled 1,300 million images everyday.

'Do a Google search' and 'Do a Yahoo search' has become part of daily life for a housewife to a researcher. In this 'Information Era' customer is 'information rich' and 'time poor'. There is an overload of information which is all pervasive. It does not matter whether it is a B2C or B2B situation. Every individual who is in need of information, be it the mailing address of a company or product information, begins with search engines. Winning on search engine optimization (SEO) seems to have become the major challenge for all—who are competing to be the 'first' in the race to provide the desired information. In this over-cluttered 'webbed world', all marketers are struggling continuously to improve their web effectiveness by delivering a meaningful, successful and, may be, joyful experience to the visitors of its website.

But in spite of the increasing importance of websites, the CEO of Jasubhai Group from India, a group which has more than 30 years of experience in managing marketing communications for B2B markets, feels that as of 2008, only 5 per cent of B2B marketers have realized the potential of online communication through websites. According to her: 'websites would become the most powerful tool for B2B communications.'

The Economics of Websites

In spite of low costs of developing the websites (a page of a website may cost as little as Rs 1,000–2,000 [US$ 2–4 per page]), a casual enquiry for the 600 SMEs based in Jamshedpur, revealed that not more than 50 would have its own website. For a 10-page website, the one time cost could be Rs 20,000 (US$ 420 @ US$ 1 = Rs 48). The annual running and maintenance cost could be around Rs 20,000 (US$ 400) per year. Very large companies like Reliance Industries, L&T, Tata Steel and Infosys may end up spending Rs 5–6 million (US$ 1–1.5 million) for the development of a 700–1,000 page website. This may not be even 0.0005 per cent of their sales. With such low expenses, websites and the Internet are goldmines at negligible costs. But the potential of these almost free goldmines is yet to be explored by majority of the B2B marketers.

Today, excellent professional help is available in India to develop very effective websites. The purpose of this chapter, in addition to a brief familiarity, is to remind the B2B marketer that websites are likely to remain the most important form of providing the information. Besides a communication platform, it can also play a critical role in building strong brands. I think that as of now, majority of the marketers have not started integrating their websites with brand-building activities.

Understanding Corporate B2B Websites' Effectiveness: Some Suggestions from the Literature

A B2B website is a gateway between a company and its prospects, customers and other stakeholders. Chakraborty et al. (2005) had identified three characteristics to judge website effectiveness. These are: informativeness; usability and quality of information.

According to Chakraborty et al. (2005), the ability of website to make a visitor feel that the it has communicated something of value is viewed as one of the most important predictors of website effectiveness. This would happen when a corporate website scores high on all the three characteristics.

These authors defined 'informativeness' as the ability of a website to make information available. Usability of information, on the other hand, reduces consumers' search costs by helping to access the information available on a website more efficiently. It is related to users' perceived ability to utilize the information provided by the website. Usability is critical in converting site visitors from 'lookers' to 'buyers'. In other words, usability at a website influences the website effectiveness. The author postulated that:

- Higher the level of perceived informativeness in a corporate website, the higher is the website's effectiveness.
- Higher the level of perceived usability in a corporate website, the higher is the website's effectiveness.
- Higher the level of perceived information quality in a corporate website, higher is the website's effectiveness.

Like the views of Chakraborty et al. (2005), are the suggestions of many regarding the meaning of website effectiveness. A Google search would reveal many such articles.

The Status of B2B Websites

A Dutch SEO company, Indenty, in its whitepaper on the effectiveness of B2B websites, found out that only 1 per cent of the 200 websites under research was doing a good job as an effective B2B website.

Its conclusion was that the majority of the websites could meet only 33 per cent of the criteria to become effective. Similarly, findings of the Kapston (2009) research (a digital marketing company based in India) on Indian websites brought out that 95 per cent of Indian B2B websites fail the usability and user experience test. The study analysed Indian companies, both large and SMEs. According to the study, majority of the corporate websites failed to provide the necessary information for stakeholders. The study also shared that websites of B2C companies are superior than that of B2B companies. Major lacunae of these websites was insufficiency of information.

According to the same study, the following appear to be the barriers to a better looking and usable website.

- Lack of knowing the importance: 42 per cent
- Lack of quality internal resource: 65 per cent; Inappropriate technology: 30 per cent; Budget unavailability: 37 per cent; Resistance/buy-in/politics within company: 55 per cent; Information technology bottleneck: 27 per cent; Lack of knowledge: 16 per cent

The Evaluation of B2B Websites: The XLRI Study

An evaluation of 50 companies mainly operating in B2B marketing was done on the 29 features of 'first impression' and 'suitability in the B2B context' around mid-2009. The combined findings are shared in Tables 8.1 and 8.2. The assessment is only about the presence and absence of features. It is not a critical evaluation of the contents and their quality.

How the Websites Faired on the Criteria: Findings of XLRI Study

1. Only seven out of the 50 companies studied have 60 per cent of all the 29 features to assess the websites. None have all the 29 features.

Table 8.1   Evaluation on First Impression

S. No.	Features of the Websites	Number with the Features	Percentage
1.	Sitemap	8	16
2.	Always visible search function	21	42
3.	Overview of products and services	21	42
4.	Text which is easy to scan	20	40
5.	Enough branding	21	42
6.	Simple and consistent navigation	30	60
7.	Availability of logo of the company	45	90
8.	Website which is up-to-date	26	58
9.	Use of images	24	48
10.	Readable text	45	90
11.	Response time	38	76
12.	Browser compatibility	23	46

Table 8.2   Suitability for the B2B Market

S. No.	Features of the Websites	Number with the Features	Percentage
1.	Testimonials	15	30
2.	Whitepapers or technical papers	12	24
3.	Online demos or trials	5	10
4.	Cases about servicing the clients	11	22
5.	Availability of newsletters	2	4
6.	Technical product information	22	44
7.	Information about servicing the clients, complains and support	8	16
8.	References	10	20
9.	Links to content on other websites	15	30
10.	Availability of instructive content	6	12
11.	Language support	6	12
12.	Encouragement of direct communication	10	20
13.	Comparison with competitors	3	6
14.	Detailed information about the company	32	64
15.	Feedback	12	24
16.	SEO	38	76
17.	Contact details	40	80

2. Eighty-four per cent of the websites do not have a sitemap and 58 per cent do not have an in-built search function. This may lead to users taking more time to locate the needed information.

3. Almost 60 per cent of the websites do not showcase their products attractively enough. This may fail to impress the prospective clients.

4. More than 70 per cent of the websites do not include whitepapers or technical papers. These may help in building credibility of the company and the products.

5. Almost 60 per cent of the websites have low browser compatibility.

6. More than 80 per cent of the websites do not offer testimonials from customers. These would be helpful in selling and branding activities.

7. Almost 90 per cent of the websites do not have multi-language support. This could help in enlarging the client base beyond English.

8. More than 70 per cent of the websites do not have a proper mechanism to handle customer feedback and complaints. Missing the feedback at no cost reflects poorly on the firm's ability to seek good payoffs from their websites.

9. Almost 50 per cent of the websites do not properly update all necessary information. Perhaps this is the most neglected aspect of website management. Recency is a major challenge for the websites.

The findings of the XLRI study, like the earlier two studies, indicate that enormous scope exists for the B2B marketers to improve their websites.

Examples of Good and Bad Websites

While sharing their presentations, on good and bad websites, a group of students specializing in B2B marketing, identified four attributes which they felt were important to judge the performance of any website. After evaluating more than 15 websites, the group shared their 'Good' and 'Bad' websites. Their evaluation is shown in Table 8.3.

Table 8.3 Attributes of Good and Bad Websites

S. No.	Attributes	Traits of a Good Website	Traits of a Bad Website
1.	System quality	• Immediate loading • Easy to navigate • Excellent search facility • Interactive multimedia	• Unorganized navigation • No search tool
2.	Information quality	• Organized in segments • Regularly updated information • Accurate information • Relevant information provided	• Disorganized information with no categorization • Lack of information under all sections
3.	Service quality	• Ownership • Trust generating • Thorough contact and feedback information • Overall well-knitted website	• Lack of ownership of brand • No feedback/responsive option • Lack of assurance of quality and safety • Overall substandard maintenance level
4.	Attractiveness	• Interesting flash animations for interactivity • Very well laid out website with grid system • Legible fonts	• Poorly rendered images • Lack of colour harmony • Inconsistency in fonts and legibility

As can be seen from the table, an effective and good website reflects inclusion of several user-friendly attributes which could make user experience pleasant and meaningful.

Websites and Brand Building

A mid-level executive working with the corporate division of a well-known global pharmaceutical company expressed his frustration that so far no organization, according to him, has made any attempt to integrate the brand-building activities with their websites. He summed up his 10-year-plus experience with digital media as the following: 'Website as a communication tool is widely known, less understood by the majority and least used as brand-building tools by any organization.' According to him, there is a long way before websites would get integrated into brand-building activities. On the other hand, a senior researcher working with the Internet research centre of a leading communication school in Singapore, shared that her experience in developing and managing websites brings out that so far there is no way to establish that a good or a bad website could have a positive or negative impact on the brand image of the organization owning the website. These two views reflect the dilemma which organizations seem to be facing.

So far, I have shared the issues pertaining to the importance and effectiveness of websites in a stand-alone manner. However, my main purpose of this chapter is to examine the role and efficacy of websites in brand building. As shared earlier, my interactions with the professionals and research brings out the fuzziness of the state of affairs. One way to bring clarity is to evaluate the website's relative role and effectiveness for a limited communication objective like creating awareness, providing information, providing sales leads, closing the sales and so on. In this sense, its effectiveness should be linked to its role to perform the desired task. This would be too narrow a view of this omnibus communication vehicle. My own suggestion is to visualize the website as a comprehensive document in digital form available to all for 24 hours. This comprehensive document could be a substitute for company's product brochures, PR material, annual reports and many more.

For long, i.e., even before the dawn of the Internet era, the brand communication pundits have been advocating for integrated communication for branding activities. If this was possible with tangible communication elements, I see no reason as to why similar attempts and expectations could not be there for the digital media like a website. A beginning has to be made to ensure good experience from the websites. This would reinforce the brand experience of all the stakeholders and help B2B marketers to strengthen their branding activities.

Summing Up

Over the years, B2B websites are showing signs of improvements. As Andy Rogers, MD, ETV Media Group online, says:

> Traditionally B2B sites have been glorified brochures. These are poorly architected information repositories with lip-service paid to design and user interface. The usage tends to be confined to information delivery with little thought paid to collecting information from customers or providing a tailored service to clients. (Blyth 2008)

I fully endorse Roger's views.

Even by 2009, my guess is that this would be true for millions and millions of B2B websites. In spite of the limitations and inadequacies, experts also feel that B2B marketers are becoming more sophisticated in their understanding of the Internet, and are showing greater concern to manage their websites. There is increasing recognition that by creating brand awareness and brand knowledge websites can contribute to building brand equity.

All websites have a potential to remain very dynamic and interactive. But the unfortunate aspect is that majority of the B2B marketers do not devote time and effort to revisit and reform their websites. After putting in substantial effort in the creation of the website, the initial enthusiasm disappears. Some of them do not remember when they created their own website. Some do not even remember when they visited their website last. For majority, it seems to have become a mere 'billboard' on the 'information highway' which no one notices.

Annexure

Table 8A.1   List of Companies: Websites Evaluated

S. No.	Websites Evaluated	S. No.	Websites Evaluated
1.	L&T	26.	Telcon
2.	Punj Llyod	27.	JCB
3.	TCS	28.	Tata
4.	TRF	29.	RIL
5.	McNally Bharat	30.	Idea
6.	Simplex	31.	Caterpillar
7.	Hewlett-Packard	32.	Kirloskar
8.	Accenture	33.	Cummins
9.	Airtel	34.	Mahindra and Mahindra
10.	Reliance Communication	35.	BSNL
11.	IBM	36.	Tata Communications
12.	HCL	37.	SKF
13.	Wipro	38.	Bajaj Bearings
14.	Stemcor	39.	Durga Bearings
15.	Tata Steel	40.	NBC Bearings
16.	Metal Junction	41.	Microsoft
17.	Cargill Steel	42.	SAP
18.	GE	43.	Emco
19.	Siemens	44.	Telk
20.	ABB	45.	Mitsubishi
21.	Areva	46.	Crompton Greaves
22.	Oracle	47.	C&S Electric
23.	Mistral	48.	Havells
24.	Norton	49.	Dell
25.	Adobe	50.	Sun

IV

Holistic Brand Management

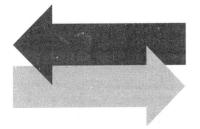

9

*Any damn fool can put on a deal but it takes genius, faith and
perseverance to create a brand.*

—David Ogilvy

〰〰　〰〰

*Excellence in execution is extremely important since brands are
built on product or service.*

—N.R. Narayana Murthy

9

Holistic Brand Management: Six Cases of B2B Brands

Brand management gurus suggest that a holistic approach (Kotler and Pfoertsch 2006: 16) is the best way for understanding the key factors that underlie a brand's success. This requires everything from the development of the product design to implementation of marketing programmes to remain synchronized on a sustained basis.

The six cases discussed in this chapter deal with brands that are acknowledged leaders in their respective fields. They reflect a very strong orientation of a holistic approach. All reflect a very imaginative use of brand-building elements. These are: Sintex, L&T Motor Starter MK1, Tata Steel's brand Structura of tubes, L&T Eutectic Alloys, OTIS elevators in India and Elgi Equipments.

Brand Sintex: Active Thinking

Converting commodity into a brand

'Intel Inside' has been quoted by a large majority of brand gurus as an outstanding success story of an intermediary B2B brand. Writers like Scott Bedbury (2002: 5) have gone to the extent of declaring a highly technically advanced and sophisticated product like a computer chip to be similar to commodities. Bedbury's argument was that products like chips (Intel) and sneakers (Nike), to begin with, were commodities for long. Both Intel and Nike can take the credit of converting these commodity situations to the world's most talked about brands. Intel, through a process of 'creative destruction' and self-cannibalization strategies, has created substantial competitive advantage. Converting a commodity into a brand is the ultimate dream and wish of every marketer. Intel and Nike seemingly have achieved their dreams. If 'Intel Inside' is an outstanding story of a global brand, the honours of a similar success in India could belong to Sintex. It is my assessment that no other brand in India including Lifebuoy,[1] the largest selling brand of soap in the world, would enjoy similar visibility as Sintex tanks sitting on the roof tops. The entire skyline of India from metros to towns to villages—be it residential or office buildings—have black plastic water tanks. These were introduced by Sintex in 1977. In spite of intense competition, Sintex enjoys 45 per cent plus market share even by mid-2009.

Introduced in late 1977, as an alternative to save the fledgling plastic division, the decision to use the plastic moulding technology to produce and market the water tank could be considered a revolutionary decision of Dangayach, the newly appointed young general manager (in 1977) of the plastic division. The promoters, Patels, had set up a plastic moulding unit to manufacture plastic tanks for the textile industry. These were to carry cotton slivers in plastic cans. But company did not succeed in marketing these cans.

This forced Patels and Dangayach to think of other end products. But even these failed to make the new investment viable. Dangayach and his team then felt the need to identify an end use with a larger market potential. This gave birth to the idea of entering into manufacturing of plastic water tanks. With this, the plant turnover, which was only Rs 0.3 million in 1975, reached the break-even sales of Rs 6 million by 1977. Today, with a turnover of nearly Rs 4,000 million, 'Sintex' has become synonymous to water tanks in India. This is a situation similar to Xerox becoming a popular term for photocopying throughout the world.

India by 2008 had around 25,000 plus plastic processing units (CMIE Prowess Database 2009). More than 90 per cent would belong to tiny and small sectors producing commodity kind of products.

In 1975, i.e., the year Patels set up the plastic manufacturing unit, the number of small and medium sectors could have been around 15,000. Like these, Patels could have remained an unknown entity. Patels and Dangayach's decision to brand their plastic containers as Sintex turned out to be a master stroke. But for the success of Sintex water tanks, even Bharat Vijay Mills, which started in 1931 in Kalol, a small town, 30 kilometres away from Ahmedabad as textile mills, could have remained an unknown textile mill of India.

The name Sintex came from 'sintering', a process of manufacturing plastic cans. Sintex combines both: the Sintering process of plastic tanks and textiles. As claimed by Dangayach, it was easy to pronounce and easy to recall. By the early 1990s, the brand Sintex became much bigger than the original textile business of the Patels. So in 1995, the Patels changed the name of their company to Sintex Industries Limited (SIL; see Bansal 2008: 302).

There is Sintex in every Indian's life

As shared by Dangayach:

> Sintex is not a luxury brand. It is for all: from low income group to high income group. We want our products to be perceived as good value for money alternatives. These plastic products are newer solutions appropriate for the Indian economy. With these, we want to make a positive difference in our customer's life. A continuous process of challenging the conventional products helps us to innovate. This way we are innovating several meaningful products and solutions. (personal communication with the author)

By 2008, Sintex had become a much diversified company. Its product mix included 20 product categories and some 3,500 products. Figure 9.1 provides the sample of products.

Its competitive advantage lay in owning 12 different plastic moulding technologies and rapid pace of product innovations. Its customer base, besides government customers, includes several well-known names, both within India and outside. Sintex had restructured its business around three broad categories. These were building products (42 per cent of sales), customer moulding (46 per cent of sales) and hi-end textiles (12 per cent of sales). These catered to the end user segments like:

Figure 9.1   Sample of Sintex Products

Source: Corporate Communication Department of Sintex.

- Water and waste management
- Affordable housing solutions
- Prefab construction
- Electrical engineering solutions
- Modern material handling

Sustaining the brand Sintex

Dangayach has been the main architect for Sintex over three decades. 'Brand should always remain youthful and vigorous. Through a continuous process of product innovations—a brand can live forever,' these were the words of Dangayach in a seminar on B2B brands in Mumbai in 2002.

Dangayach feels that building individual brands for each product category would be very expensive. Elaborating further he shared:

> Our size of business with sales of Rs 17,000 million in 2008, may not be able to support individual brands for each and every product category. Huge amount would be sunk to build the individual brands. The individual product market size is not large enough to support the creation of individual brands. It is my view that for B2B markets, brand gives a macro level support. But for success, a strong name is not enough. Besides the product quality and technology, the commercial dimensions too play an important role in the success of a brand.

Reflecting on future challenges, Dangayach felt that Sintex has a very strong image as a water tank company. The name has become synonymous to the product category, i.e., plastic tanks. Now the other product categories which may enjoy similar visibility are the plastic 'enclosures' for energy metres and other electrical items.

For the year 2007–08, Sintex's total marketing spend on sales of Rs 17,000 millions was around Rs 250 million, i.e., 1.5 per cent of sales. Looking at the impact it seems that the company has managed its communication spend exceedingly well.

Besides this, Sintex also has a website which provides the details of the company and its product line. The website, according to Dangayach, is a strong brand-building tool. Reflecting on how he succeeded in making Sintex a global brand, Dangayach shared that Sintex does some brand-building activities for the original equipment (OE) customers and the financers. But to build a global brand for household consumers in foreign countries would be beyond the brand-building strategy of Sintex. It does not have the resources and this is not required since its global customers comprise of essentially automobile component manufacturers.

By 2008, Sintex had acquired three companies abroad. All these have some well-known auto manufacturers as their clients. This, Dangayach felt, would provide experience to serve the global customers and gain insights to develop global brands.

B2B vs B2C customers

Dangayach feels that a key difference between B2B and B2C customers is that whereas a B2B customer can always measure performance, this may not be possible in several B2C situations. B2C customers mainly go on the basis of feel and touch. But ability to measure performance does not mean that brands have no role in B2B markets. Our performance over the years vindicates that a strong brand plays an important role even in a commodity kind of situation. But a strong brand alone may not result into a successful business performance. 'At the end, the product must deliver the promise,' feels Dangayach.

Corporate social responsibility: The green Sintex

Sintex's claim to be an environment-friendly company comes from its advocacy to use plastics in buildings. These products are window frames, doors, composites and pre-fabricated buildings of plastics. It claims that plastic doors and windows are energy saving options. The door partitions, false ceilings, wall panelling, cabins, cabinets, etc., have significantly contributed in reducing deforestation and saving the use of wood.

By designing and creating several useful products and systems that addresses collection, transfer and composting of municipal solid waste, Sintex is also closely committed to keep cities and towns clean. As commitment to keep environment clean, Sintex had installed 20,000 pre-fabricated toilets at the famous 'Kumbh Mela' of Allahabad.

For several years Sintex has been working on biogas plants made from plastics. Due to its efforts, there is now a realization that the small-sized pre-fab or factory-made biogas plant is the answer to accelerate the biogas programme. Similarly, Sintex is working with the Ministry of New and Renewable Energy to develop models that can work not only in rural but urban areas as well.

Sintex: An innovative brand forever

In the year 1980, the sale of Sintex was merely Rs 78 million. Till 1996–97, sales growth was slow and it was barely Rs 1,480 million. In the next 10 years, i.e., by 2005–06, it reached Rs 8,750 million (Sintex 2005–09). But by 2008, i.e., within three years it has nearly doubled to Rs 17,000 million. What seemed to be slow and incremental for decades is now galloping. It has plans to reach Rs 50,000 million in the next three years. The journey which began in 1975 to manufacture plastic tanks has, by 2009, more than 3,500 products belonging to 20 product categories. As claimed by the management, if Sintex was not a strong brand, it would not have been able to achieve a success rate of nearly 60 per cent for its new range of innovative products as against a mere 10–15 per cent of the success rate of new products world over. Instead of confining to India, Sintex now boasts of presence in nine countries across four continents. Most of its customers are global giants and are part of Fortune 500 Companies.

Reflecting its concern for environment and India, it proudly claims its association in developing India by providing solutions to key sectors. These are housing sanitation, power and education sectors. Instead of being known for producing mere plastic products, it wants to be known as 'thinking company' producing innovative products which save the environment.

Motor Starter Type MK1 of L&T

L&T is the largest engineering and construction conglomerate of India. It began its operation in 1938. The promoters were two Danish Engineers—Henning Holck-Larsen and S.K. Toubro. In the last 70 years, the company has become a giant in almost all its business in India. Its combined revenues for the financial year 2007–08 were around Rs 270,000 million (US$ 5 billion). In Chapter 5, I have shared as to how L&T has become a strong corporate brand. This case deals with a specific product category. The product category belongs to the Electrical Business Group (EBG). The total product mix of EBG is: Switch gear Products, Electrical Systems, Metering Solutions and Relays, Medical Equipment and Systems, Control and Automation, Petroleum Dispensers and Tooling Solutions. By 2007, the sales of EBG were around Rs 24,000 million, i.e., 9 per cent of the total sales of L&T (L&T 2007).

The Electrical Standard Product Group

Electrical Standard Product (ESP) is a very important group of EBG. The ESP accounted for nearly 50 per cent of the total sales of EBG. It has a very wide and deep range of products for low voltage (upto 440 volts) operations. These include air circuit breakers, moulded case circuit breakers, switch fuse units, miniature circuit breakers, switches, electrical cables, energy measurement metres, and so on. These products could be used in homes as well as in factories. The customers could be the building promoters, power producing companies, machinery producing companies and the farmers. The first product of the ESP group was an electrical motor starter for agriculture pumps introduced in the mid-1950s. This was popularly known as LT-LK starter. This motor starter has a very old technology (electro mechanical and gravity operated).

But even by 2008, it remained a favourite of the Indian farmers. By 2008, ESP had sold more than 10 million starters to farmers. ESP had made several attempts to drop this product due to the use of outdated technology but farmers and stockist prevented them to drop it. (In 2007, the LT-LK-make starter had sales revenue of Rs 800 million [US\$ 20 million].) This starter for farmers (used in the agriculture sector) provided an excellent opportunity to ESP to use mass media like radio and TV for several decades. These promotions helped L&T to create awareness not only for its starters but also about itself as a company. Through promotions in All India Radio (A.I.R.) (the only option to the marketers till the time FM radio channel started in the late 1990s) and the government-controlled Doordarshan (TV channel) up to the late 1980s, L&T became a widely-known company amongst common public, both customers and non-customers. Had this starter for farmers not been there, L&T promotions and communication would have remained confined to its business customers, preventing a high public visibility of L&T.

The competition

By the end of 2007, the products of ESPs were competing with several well-known MNCs like Siemens, Schindler, ABB and GE. In spite of being very large and dominant global players, none could come near to the market shares of L&T. For most of its products, ESP enjoyed market shares varying from 40–50 per cent. These competitors were able to get a premium of nearly 25 per cent over L&T products outside India, but could not do so within India.

The organization of marketing function of ESP

In 2005, the ESP division set a very ambitious sales growth target of 40 per cent. It realized that new market segments and new products would be needed to achieve this ambitious growth. It also recognized that till 2005, ESP was essentially dominant in only two segments, 'agriculture' (starters like LT-LK) and 'industries'. The industry segment included manufacturing organizations like steel, automobile, cement, textiles, chemicals, and so on. The reformulated strategy identified five dominant segments for ESP. These were:

1. Industry: All manufacturing organizations like steel, chemicals, engineering, and so on.
2. Buildings: Building promoters, construction firms and individual household customers.
3. OEM: These include manufacturers of textile machinery, machine tools, construction machinery and many more.
4. Agriculture: Farmers and businesses like tea gardens, orchards, and so on.
5. Utility companies: These include electrical power producing companies in public and private sectors like Tata Power, Gujarat State Electricity Board, and so on.

In order to follow a segmented approach, a new organizational structure was conceived by ESP. Besides the five segments mentioned, the five dominant product groups of ESP are shown in Table 9.1.

Table 9.1   The Product Mix of ESP

Product Description	Some Indicative Products
1. Power gear	Air Circuit Breakers (ACB), Moulded Case Circuit Breakers (MCCB), Switch Discontinuing Fuses (SDFs)
2. Control gear	Contactors and relays
3. Energy management	Energy metres, protection relays, capacitors
4. Final distribution products	Wires, cables, wiring accessories, switches, automation products
5. Agricultural products	Starters

Figure 9.2 provides a glimpse of the product mix.

The brand-building efforts

ESP has different sets of activities for each segment. Thus, for the building segment, ESP conducts training camps for electricians and roadshows in the electrical markets of major cities. Approximately

Figure 9.2   The Product Mix of ESP

Source: Corporate Communication Department of L&T.

50–70 electricians are trained in each camp. Each branch has a target of conducting five to seven training camps per year. In all, there are 30 branches. Imparting knowledge is the key concern for these camps. Besides classroom inputs, the electricians get free lunch and a small gift. ESP wishes to continue these activities on a sustained basis to reinforce the brand recall and recognition.

In order to motivate the stockist each year ESP organizes a conference, outside India, of 100 top performers (around July 2008, ESP had nearly 700 stockists).

ESP provides several points of purchase for display materials like dangles, signages, and so on, in the shops and offices of the stockist. It also regularly monitors these displays to ensure standardization throughout India.

In order to display the entire range of various products, ESP books space with stockist in the electrical markets of the metros. The plan is to have these exclusive product displays in all the metros of India.

Advertisements in select trade journals are another important promotional activity of ESP. Magazines such as *Purchase, Search, Electrical, Monitor* and *Industrial Product Finder* are important and popular. Recently, ESP has also been signed with 'Home Town' initiative of Pantaloon. ESP had booked space in Ahmedabad, Lucknow and Noida (in Uttar Pradesh).

ESP has also tied-up with the electrical departments of 40 leading engineering colleges of India. In these, ESP displays its product range. The colleges have to provide 200–300 square feet of space. ESP supplies all material free to these colleges.

For 'agri' segment

This would essentially be a situation of B2C marketing. For this, ESP has been organizing farmers meet on a regular basis. These are done through mobile vans. Besides product knowledge, farmers are also given some free gifts. In addition to publicity through mobile vans and farmers meet, ESP also uses the regional TV and radio channels. For the agriculture segments, ESP also participates in two large exhibitions, one in Ludhiana and another in Pune every year.

For industry segment

ESP participates in 'Elecrama', a trade show of Indian Electrical and Electronics Manufacturers Association (IEEMA). This is held every alternate year and ESP has been participating regularly in this trade show for long. These help ESP to showcase its product range including new products. This has helped ESP in managing its brand presence and leadership.

For building segment

Recognizing the importance of the consultants and architects, ESP invites them to its service centre in Coonoor (a hill resort, near Ooty). These visits are organized three to four times a year. Each seminar may have around 25–30 participants. This way it is able to cover 100–150 top ranking consultants and architects. ESP also participates in two exhibitions in a year, one held in Mumbai and another in Delhi

Factory visits

It is ESP's view that visits to the factory are the most effective form of brand building. Each year, nearly 300 people visit the factories. These visits are round the year and a dedicated team of ESP takes care of these visits. These visitors could be electrical consultants, customers, architects or machinery manufacturers.

Websites

ESP feels that substantial scope exists to make websites an effective media for a two-way communication. Currently the website of the company is handled by the Corporate Communication department of the head office.

Training centres

These have been recognized as a very important aspect of brand building and product promotion. By July 2008, ESP had three training centres located in Pune, Lucknow and Coonoor in the south. Recognizing that not much is either taught or known in the field of low voltage (upto 440 volts), ESP created these training centres to promote good electrical engineering practices. The objective was not product promotion but to impart knowledge for the selection and maintenance of electrical equipment. ESP recognized that neither the engineers nor diploma holders, including the electricians, had any knowledge of the products of ESP. These training programmes generate substantial goodwill which could then be cashed by the sales engineers of ESP.

Besides training the raw and less experienced, ESP has been using these training centres to host seminars for top consultants. These seminars cover the trends in technological developments. They also help in conveying to these consultants that ESP (L&T) is at par or may be ahead of the MNCs. These, in this sense, also help in improving the technical image of ESP and L&T. Each seminar invites 25–30 consultants. In the last four years, ESP has covered more than 300 electrical consultants who could be both the specifiers and influencers for the selection of the electrical products.

These training centres also conduct programmes for the students from engineering colleges, polytechnics and industrial training institutes. These students are exposed to the world of switch gear: contactors, relays, switch boards, and so on. The number of students in a year could be very large.

The initial expense to set up these training centres was around Rs 30 million for each training centre. None of ESP's competitors have these kinds of training centres.

The service centres

Besides 700 stockists and three training centres, ESP has also created 100 service centres throughout India. These are independent franchisees. They provide preventive regular maintenance through Annual Maintenance Contracts (AMC) and also attend to the breakdown. Each service centre has two to three persons who provide great assurance to the customers through quality service. To support these, ESP also has 45 service engineers.

Another brand-building activity of ESP is its initiative of free health check-ups for women and children residing in villages. The local branches have tied-up with local doctors. The branch members also distribute free books and stationery items. (Currently L&T's ESP is present in 275 out of the 600-odd districts in India.)

The segments and effective promo tools

Commenting upon the effectiveness of promo tools for various segments, a senior manager shared the following as shown in Table 9.2.

Table 9.2   Effectiveness of Promo Tools

Segment	Most Effective Promo Tools
1. OE customers	Product clinics and advertising in trade journals
2. Industrial customers	In-plant training of personnel and seminars
3. Agriculture sector	Free service camps and van campaigning

Summing up

The practice of ESP suggests that brand building is multifaceted. There are several options available but sustenance of these initiatives is the key. Backed up by strong quality products, the ESP branding initiatives have enabled achieving market shares of nearly 50 per cent of its dominant product lines. The strong brand of L&T's ESP is also being leveraged for its new products and new segments.

Brand Structura: Revolutionizing the Indian Construction Scenario

Steel tubes have several end uses. These include conveyance of water, steam, gas and oil. The other end uses are for the automotive products like cars, trucks, motor cycles and bicycles. Besides these, another end use of steel tubes has been in the construction of industrial sheds and buildings. Each end use requires a specialized product. Thus, tubes carrying water are classified as commercial tubes. For more than 50 years, the tubes division of Tata Steel had enjoyed the widest product mix catering to all the end user segments. Figures 9.3 and 9.4 provide a view and use of Brand Structura. By 2000, the share of commercial tubes was approximately 70 per cent of the total sales. Around 2004, the tubes division started witnessing stagnancy in sales. An important reason was the increasing popularity of plastic tubes. Against tubes division aspirations of 20 per cent annual growth, it was witnessing a growth rate of only 2 per cent. The tubes division felt that a radically innovative approach for the hollow sections could change the fortune of the division and help in achieve growth objectives.

The Brand Structura: Pre-launch analysis

The focus group discussions with architects and construction engineers surfaced that the architects and Indian customers were aware of the heavy use of hollow sections in construction outside India. But its use was very limited in India. A major bottleneck was

Figure 9.3   Butterfly Park, Bangalore

Source: Corporate Communication Department of Tata Steel.

Figure 9.4   Mumbai Airport

Source: Corporate Communication Department of Tata Steel.

the inability of the architects and designers to use the hollow sections due to lack of knowledge about specifications and availability of accessories. Unlike in the West, the Indian architects also lacked the exposure of several additional end uses of hollow sections in the entire construction space. As visualized by the tubes division, the scope was very wide. These were very well captured by the 'Solution Centres' of the steel hollow section manufacturers of the developed economies like the USA and Western Europe.

Exposure and a challenge by the MD of Tata Steel to revamp the sales of hollow sections became one of the major motivators to launch the hollow sections under the brand name 'Structura' in December 2005. Besides 'branding' the product, the tube division also reorganized its marketing around four segments of construction markets. These were:

- Infrastructure
- Industrial
- Architectural
- General engineering

The infrastructure segments comprised organizations like Airport Authority of India (AAI), Railways Design and Standard Organization (RDSO, Lucknow), National Highway Authority of India (NHAI), and so on.

The industrial customers were essentially the manufacturing and service industries in need of industrial sheds. Their number could be very large. The architectural segment included situations where steel tubular structures could be used in activities like fancy gate, garage, canopy, and so on. General engineering could include several end uses. One important end use was for scaffolding. The demand for this end use alone, according to the executives, was likely to be huge.

The brand-building effort

Several networking and partnership arrangements were activated by the tubes division to make Structura a strong brand. The final objective was to create demand by enabling greater and greater use of Structura. For this, it re-vamped its distribution network by appointing 11–12 business development partners. They screened and reduced the size of its distributors from 120 to 80. The selected business partners had to play an active role in generating demand for Structura. This required changing their mindset from simply selling tubes like any commodity to market development activity through pre-sales activities. The tubes division also began strengthening its relationship with consultants and engineers through out India. It also hired two specialists to create knowledge and information to help the customers and consultants to promote the use of Structura.

Partnership with IA&B played a very pivotal role in the brand-building activity of Structura. With their help, the tubes division organized a contest for designers and architects titled 'Notions of Nation'. In all, 400 architects participated. Regional juries selected the top three architects from each region. The designs of winners were shown through mobile exhibition which displayed them in important consumption centres for two to three days. Besides building up relationship with the architects and designers, the tubes division, through this contest was also keen to demonstrate endless possibilities of using Structura in structures. It also wanted to communicate the benefits of using Structura. These were: reduction in the usage of steel by 15–20 per cent as contrast to steel in concrete; reduction in project construction time and also improved aesthetics of the buildings. It could also communicate unlocking of innovativeness and imagination in the design of shapes of several buildings and their facades with the use of Structura.

Another initiative of the tubes division was to set up 'Structura Studios'. As the architects want everything in one place, these studios could be the one-stop knowledge hubs.

The tubes division also shared that a business development partner, who had opened the Structura studio only six months back, is now getting orders for turn key jobs using Structura.

The developments post Structura

The head of Marketing shared that in 2004, the tubes division was selling around 200,000 tons of all types of tubes per annum. Its sales revenues were Rs 7 billion. By 2008, the target was to achieve a sale of 360,000 tons and a sales revenue of Rs 15 billion. He shared that a 50 per cent increase in the sales would be on account of Structura. This implied a growth rate of 40 per cent per annum for Structura. This remarkable performance of hollow sections could have not been possible, if they were not branded as 'Structura'.

Challenges for future

The executives of tubes division identified several challenges to ensure sustenance of the performance of Structura. These were:

- How to convert the thinking of the fabricators as majority of them feel comfortable in using conventional materials like 'steel angles' and channels.
- Newer ideas for 'value creation' by using Structura. This may require strengthening the service package from the 'service centres' of Structura.
- Whether the tubes division should enter into the business of designing and providing solutions. An example of this could be the design and construction of complete airports. This would tantamount to competing with its clients like GMR construction, L&T or Gammon India.
- Inspite of the future challenges and possibilities, the tube division is very bullish about Structura's future. It feels that India is currently in the 'evolving' stage with huge pent up demand. Creation of solution centres like Corus can provide the impetus to accelerate the demand for Structura.

Summing up

Hollow tubular section has been in the product mix up of the tubes division for more than 30 years. In spite of several selling efforts, the sales remained insignificant till early 2005. Branding helped in unleashing the hidden potential of this sleeping giant in India. Today every major project, be it of airports, huge office complexes like that of Infosys in Pune and Mysore, a sports complex or stations of Delhi Metro Railways, all have become impressive testimonials of brand Structura. But these are early days of Structura in India. As claimed by the tubes division, the use is still evolving. Brands energize the organizations. This is what it has done to the 50-year-old tubes division of Tata Steel.

L&T Eutectic: The Low Heat Welding Electrodes

Eutectic Alloys are used to reclaim and reuse the expensive parts of engines, earth moving equipments like bulldozers, excavators, buckets, engine heads of the cars and trucks, mines and machinery equipments, structures, and so on. The end use situations could run into millions. At a fraction of the cost of the new part or component, the customer could reclaim and reuse these with the help of the welding alloys. In order to help the customer, L&T Eutectic employs a very large number of application engineers. These engineers are located at all the important consumption sectors. These could be large metros to remote areas in coal belts of Jharkhand, Nagpur and many more.

Around the mid-1990s, the then GM, Marketing, Eutectic Alloys, had a team of around 300 application engineers. The customer base being wide and scattered all over India required the use of distributors/dealers (channel members). In all, Eutectic Alloys had around 210 hundred-channel partners. At this time, the industry was growing at the rate of 10–15 per cent per annum. Against this, the GM set an ambitious growth target of 26 per cent per year to double the sales every three years. This growth, which was almost double the industry growth, appeared to be a very daunting task to the team. Even to his boss, the growth appeared to be very ambitious. The GM, however, went ahead to achieve the tough targets set by him.

The brand-building initiatives

Achievement of ambitions demanded ways and means to improve the productivity of both the GM's sales team and the channel partners. Figure 9.5 shows his conceptualization regarding formulation of the action plans.

Figure 9.5   The Integrative Triangle

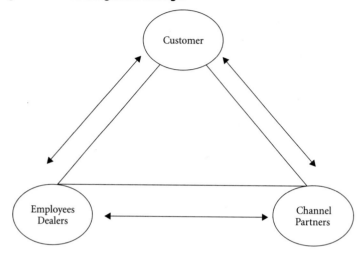

Source: Author.

Armed with this integrated view, his action plan included simultaneous action on the three areas.

The employees

Accelerating the growth in sales needed improvements in the productivity of application engineers. A major challenge was the sustenance of motivation of the team of 300 application engineers located in remote places which were both away from the home and the head office. The GM visualized that an in-house magazine, published regularly and circulated to the family members could play an important role. Regular sharing of the news like revision of sales targets, achievements and rewards to the application engineers could create awareness about the company amongst the family members. Their awareness could help them to motivate the application engineers to perform better. As pointed out by him, the competitive spirit amongst application engineers, in which their families were the motivators, had a direct bearing on the achievement of the ambitious targets.

Faster sharing of knowledge amongst the engineers was critical to gain competitive advantage. For this the GM provided all his 300 application engineers with laptops. These could be connected through Wide Area Network (WAN). This not only enabled connectivity, but also helped in storing and sharing of the knowledge for thousands of solutions used by the application engineers to solve problems of the customers. Though equipping each and every engineer with a laptop was a very expensive idea, but the productivity gains were substantial. Earlier, knowledge of each application remained either in the mind of application engineer or in their files. To retrieve these was very time consuming. Shortening of response time led to tremendous gains in productivity and sales.

Training of the application engineers, welders and dealers too was identified as crucial for the desired results. This not only helped in job performance, but also in boosting the self-confidence. For this, Eutectic Alloys set up a very sophisticated training institute at its headquarter in Mumbai. Besides training the existing force, this training institute is also developing new 'welders'. The training institute has also become a platform to invite the influencers and decision makers to the institute. This has enabled regular sharing of the latest developments with the influencers and decision makers. The GM shared that in 1995, the cost to set up the institute was around Rs 30 million.

The channel partners

Around the mid-1990s, Eutectic had 210 stockists. Even though associated for long, the GM's assessment was that the channel partners were keen on short term sales at any cost, rather than in providing high quality service to the customers. He further felt that channel partners did not reflect anything unique from their retail outlets. To him, these appeared to be 'run of the mill' kind of outfits. They were mainly relying on the brand pull and the support of application engineers to generate sales leads and sales. Being an important part of the value chain, the GM concluded that they needed to be invigorated at an accelerated pace. The need was to shake up their complacency. He felt that creating competition amongst dealers would help. He introduced the idea of organizing dealers meet of outstanding performers with their families outside India. Involving family—wives and children—he analysed, could be the major push. This really worked! The family was now monitoring the performance closely. Besides the contest, the magazine was totally dedicated to the channel partners—which included their family members also—and was used as a platform to share news and developments. This too helped in the transformation of the outlook of channel partners.

The customers

The GM knew that the use of Eutectic Alloys helps in recovering worn-out parts of waste and junk. He saw an opportunity in involving customers by organizing a 'conservation contest' amongst them. The highest savers were declared as winners. The saving was calculated as customers' attempt to save their parts and components as against buying a new part. Thus, as an example of a winner was BEST (the bus-operating company of Mumbai); by repairing 16,000 parts and spending Rs 2–3 million, it could save Rs 18 million.

An important dimension of enhanced customer connectivity was the increasing expectations of the customers to provide more and more technologically-advanced products. This led to the creation of an Advanced Technology Cell (ATC) to provide state-of-the-art welding alloys. This not only excited the customers but also rejuvenated the marketing team of Eutectic who were popularly known as Eutecticians.

The outcome

Eutectic's holistic brand management approach delivered excellent results. Against the growth target of 26 per cent per annum, it crossed 30 per cent per year for two consecutive years. In contrast, its nearest competitor grew only by 10 per cent. Reflecting on this outstanding performance, the GM identified motivation of his people, training of marketing team, communication to the team as well as to the stockist and changing the outlook of the channel partners from sales to service orientation as key factors in creating a strong brand L&T Eutectic.

Branding Challenges: OTIS Elevators

Elevators (popularly called as 'lifts' in India) could be amongst the most visible products in the domain of B2B markets. Besides enjoying high visibility, it is also a touch and feel product for the end users.

Born in 1853, OTIS has local roots in more than 200 countries and territories. By 2009, it had installed approximately 2.2 million elevators and escalators worldwide. It was maintaining 1.6 million elevators and escalators worldwide.[2] Elevators and escalators, over the years, have seen substantial technological advances leading to faster and smoother vertical rides. Besides the smooth and fast rides, safety is a critical component. Snapping of wire ropes, which are used to move the elevators up and down, can result in accidents. A complex system of controls and logic linked to electrical motors, pulleys, gears and a vast array of electronic items are used in controlling the movement of elevators. They play a very important role in the movement and operation of the elevators as per the commands of people to minimize the waiting time.

For millions and millions of customers, this very complex paraphernalia of what lies behind the scene means nothing. So long as elevators and escalators perform, a brand remains anonymous. But the moment it does not perform, it can lead to chaos and crisis, especially in critical places like airports, hotels, railway stations, high rise buildings hospitals and other places of public use and importance. For leaders like OTIS, it becomes a major challenge to deliver high quality performance, in every minute of product usage, in millions of installations all over the globe. The task is daunting. But seemingly it has made it appear very simple for the customers. OTIS has been able to maintain its leadership since it entered the Indian markets. OTIS service standards have been outstanding. This has happened from its inception; OTIS has defined elevators as a 'service' business and not an elevator-producing business. 'Service backed up by excellent quality products' appears to be its motto. Out of the 2,100 people employed by OTIS India in early 1990s, nearly 700 were in the manufacturing plant, roughly 700 in installation and commissioning and 700 were managing servicing of the elevators.

In 2008 service contributed to 40 per cent of its revenue in India. It was employing nearly 2,200 people, two-thirds of them being in the field operations. Its website claims that it is maintaining 40,000 elevators all over India and has presence in around 300 cities. It is still the leader and sells around 5,000 elevators per year.[3]

Even before the advent of the Internet, mobile phones and CRM packages, it had developed a highly innovative system to ensure very high standards of service even in an infrastructure-poor country like India. It would hire outsiders to do random checks on the elevators installed in different cities. These checks were done on the basis of the cards kept in 'Cardex' which provided complete details of the installation. It would also conduct customer satisfaction studies on a regular basis. To ensure that elevators do not go out of order even due to trivial reasons like cigarette butts in the groove of the door channels, improper electrical contacts or poor preventive maintenance, it had its own fleet of service personnel. It would train and maintain close relationship with the security and main-tenance staff in small buildings with one or two elevators. A city like Mumbai may account for 40 per cent of the elevators in India. This fleet of service personnel would move on motorcycles with walky-talky type of phones. They could be contacted on these by thousands of stand-alone residential building societies. This was done to ensure minimum downtime. It also provided training to the security guards regarding how to keep the engine room (housing pulleys and motors) clean. It trained them as to what to check first (similar to first aid principles), if a lift goes out of order, even before contacting the service personnel of OTIS. For five star hotels, with very high visibility and where elevators availability has to be for 365 days and 24 hours, it used to park its own engineers on the premises of these hotels.

Today, in the IT and mobile phone era, OTIS seemingly is doing all this, with more satisfaction and faster responses.

Summing up

For a visible product like elevators and escalators, the brand-building opportunities are enormous. Every manufacturer can and should visualize the payoffs at an early stage. But mere signs and logos at construction sites would not make a strong brand. A desire to make a strong brand must come at the time of setting up the business. OTIS, right from the beginning, had defined their business as more of a service rather than merely producing elevators. This orientation has delivered handsome dividends by ensuring that OTIS remains a strong global brand. If the desire or urge to create a strong brand (and this is true for all B2B products) does not come early, it would be very late, when competition would strike. Post 1991, once the Indian economy opened, several Indian and local brands of elevators disappeared.

Building Brand Elgi: A Leading Compressor Manufacturer of India

Elgi compressors have been in the business for nearly 50 years. It first began by supplying maintenance equipment for auto garages. Over the years it has become a very strong player both in India and outside. It is a close second to MNC brands like Atlas Copco (AC) and Ingersol Rand (IR). Compressors are back-end products which are practically needed for every industry from mining of iron ores to production of medicines. One can see air compressors in petrol pumps, filling air in automobiles as well as in the the golf courses helping golfers to clean their shoes. But in spite of the several end uses, compressors do not enjoy the same visibility as elevators. For more than 40 years, Elgi, as a company, though has been performing well, was maintaining a low key on its brand-building activities. However in the last 8–10 years Elgi equipments has been investing on branding activities on a sustained basis.

Reflecting on the brand Elgi, the MD shared:

> In the domestic markets, Elgi has a positive legacy. This has happened not because of hard core brand building efforts, but due to implicit brand behavior. Elgi has always been a service led organization. Elgi has never entered into any mud slinging arguments with the customers. The customer satisfaction has been always high for our products. This has been a very

strong underpinning for Elgi brand. In last 8 years, Elgi has become more explicit in its brand building efforts. It has started using mass media. It is actively participating in many trade shows and exhibitions. These are helping in brand building. (personal communication with the MD)

Recognizing that product quality is very crucial, Elgi equipments has invested heavily on R&D and technological interventions. This has helped in improving product performance. Besides investment in technology, investment in people has been identified as critical. Earlier the sales people appeared meek and submissive to the customers. But now they appear more confident, assertive and empathetic to the customers. 'The improved quality and change in the profile of our sales team has had a positive rub off on the brand image of Elgi,' shared the MD.

On a sales of Rs 3,800 million (in 2007), the advertising and communication budget for Elgi was around Rs 45 million. Elgi's spend was Rs 12 million on exhibition and trade shows in 2007. In early 2008, Elgi has started conducting roadshows on display vehicles in Chennai. The amount spend on such roadshows could be around Rs 0.2 million per roadshow. In 2008, Elgi has also used services of *Business Today*, a leading business magazine of India.

As per Elgi, the most effective vehicle for brand promotion for compressors is 'exhibition' and 'trade shows'. Participation in the Hanover Fair (in Germany), a mecca for industrial products including compressors, has helped a great deal. It costs Rs 5–6 million per fair. Twelve years back, it began with a small space of 200 square feet as stall space. By 2008, Elgi started booking 800 square feet to set up its stall. Using the German professionals to manage the stall helped a great deal in enhancing global awareness of Elgi. In its first two participations, the distributors did not appear attracted but now the stalls attract dealers from all over the globe. Today, Elgi is known within the air compressor fraternity worldwide. Though at the end-customers level, Elgi's awareness is still low, as claimed by the management, Elgi is known to at least 50–60 per cent overseas channel members. This was achieved through a focused attempt. After realizing that its image was getting diffused as a multi-product company, the management decided to become only a compressor company by exiting from all other business.

Elgi has developed its website internally. It has started appearing at the No. 1 position on Google search engines for air compressors in India. It has also been appearing at the No. 64 position on Google on a worldwide search. Earlier it would figure at 124,000 position in the search list of air compressors. It is Elgi's view that the Internet would be a phenomenal tool for B2B companies. It has yet to explore its full potential. Besides websites, exhibitions, advertising in magazines like *Business Today*, Elgi also publishes a 60-page magazine every year.

Summing up his observations, the MD shared that: 'For us, technology is the key. It's only the technology which would help us to maintain the strength of the brand.' Elgi is amongst the few global players to manufacture its own air ends. This has given Elgi tremendous competitive advantage. Globally, Elgi is present in more than 50 countries.

By 2008, Elgi had achieved a sale of Rs 5,000 million. Its global ranking would be amongst the top 20 compressor manufacturers. It is now becoming more organized and aggressive in its global operations. Besides opening offices abroad, it has also set up a manufacturing facility in China. As pointed out by the VP, Marketing, Elgi has been accepted as a major competitor by established MNCs like Atlas Copco and Ingersol Rand in India; soon they might declare Elgi as a global brand of reckoning. As mentioned earlier, its concerted efforts of the last 8–10 years are finally paying off.

Summing up

Product quality, service and good value for money coupled with effective communication plans help in creating strong brands. But more than the decisions on what needs to be done, is the firm's ability to execute what it desires to achieve. As Narayana Murthy (2009: 283) suggests: 'Excellence in execution is extremely important since brands are built on product and service experience.' Equally critical is the sustenance of the brand building activities. All the six cases demonstrate that brand-building is not only multi-faceted but needs to be sustained on a regular basis.

V

The Future Challenges

10

A flat world is a world that allows globalization to flourish.

—Narayana Murthy

~~~   ~~~

Globalization has changed us into a company that searches the world, not just to sell or to source, but to find intellectual capital—the world's best talents and greatest ideas.

—Jack Welch

10

Beyond Exports: Creating Indian Global Brands—Reality and Possibilities

'Bringing Back the Glory: Can Indian Brands Make Brand India Global?'

In the year 1000 AD, India accounted for 29 per cent of world's gross domestic product (GDP) (Gupta et al. 2008: 238). Europe's was 13 per cent and America stood only at 0.7 per cent. In 1700 AD, India's share of the world economy was 24 per cent, America's 0.2 per cent and Europe's 30 per cent. By 1820, India with 16 per cent and China with 33 per cent accounted for nearly 50 per cent of the world GDP and the US was only 2 per cent. But by 1950, America's share increased to 31 per cent, Europe's to 39 per cent, China accounted for 4.5 per cent and India only 4.2 per cent (Madison 2003). Thus, within 130 years, both China and India lost their dominance in world economy.

Likewise, in 1948–49, that is, only one year after Independence, as against world's total export of US$ 57.3 billion, India's export of US$ 1.3 billion accounted for 2.3 per cent of the world trade. By 1980–81, India's export was US$ 8.5 billion.[1] This was as low as 0.45 per cent of world's total of US$ 1,990 billion. This abysmally poor performance led many researchers and economists to ridicule India. 'No government world over, has worked as hard as Government of India to successfully bring down its contribution of global trade from 2.3 to 0.45 per cent.' Table 10.1 provides the export performance of India over the years.

Table 10.1   India and the Globe: India's Share in World Exports

Year	World Export (US$ Billion)[a]	India's Export (US$ Billion)[b]	India's Percentage Share in the World
1948–49	57.3	1.3	2.3
1960–61	129	2.2	1.7
1990	3,334.4	18.0	0.54
2003	7,425	53	0.71
2007	13,729	145	1.1

Sources: [a] WTO Report on World merchandize exports and World commercial services. Available online at http://www.wto.org/english/res_e/statis_e/its2009_e/section1_e/i06.xls; http://www.wto.org/english/res_e/statis_e/its2009_e/appendix_e/a08.xls
[b] Indiastat reports on Total Exports of India. Available online at http://www.indiastat.com/foreigntrade/12/exports/91/totalexports/17955/stats.aspx

A quick comparison with China indicates that in 1980, China and India were at par in terms of export as a percentage to GDP. It was 6 per cent for China and 7 per cent for India. But by 2005, exports were contributing 38 per cent to China's GDP and for India the exports were contributing only 21 per cent (Gupta et al. 2008: 7). In the same year, China's GDP was US$ 2,234 billion (US$ 1,700 per capita) and India's GDP was US$ 806 billion (US$ 726 per capita) (Gupta et al. 2008: 240).

One can continue to share a lot more. But the fact remains that in terms of globalization, India has been an under-performer for more than 62 years. India cannot allow this to continue. The performance has to change for better. Brand gurus like Keller suggest that Indian brands should strive to underline their presence in global markets through strong performances and competitiveness. He observed: 'In contemporary times, very often the image of a country is influenced by strong brand that achieves global leadership from that nation' (Keller 2005).

For nearly 0.3 million exporters from India,[2] Keller's views provide the aspirations and direction. The starting point would be global competitiveness and presence beyond India. A large majority of companies are aware of it. Post 1991, that is, the year of opening up of the Indian economy, several Indian companies started gaining global competitiveness. Indian companies were fast to get certifications like ISO 9000, 9001, and so on. The other was to implement practices like TPM, TQM, Six Sigma, Quality Circles, Value Engineering and lean management of Toyota Motors. They were busy toning up their process by following models similar to the Malcolm Baldrige Quality Awards of the US. IT initiatives like ERP and CRM supplemented their efforts to strengthen the processes through efficient management of information. Simultaneously, they started increasing their engagements with the global markets. Newspapers and business journals remained full of news like Tata Steel becoming the lowest cost producer of steel in the globe (Tata Steel 2009) and L&T bagging very large orders from gulf countries.[3] Following the footprints of the Indian giants were thousands and thousands of SMEs. This was getting reflected in improved performance of exports from India. In the last five years, that is., between 2003 and 2008, exports have grown at 20 per cent per annum (see Table 10.1). Some large companies had a substantial share of the exports in their annual sales. Table 10.2 provides performance of some select companies.

These increasing exports prompted Arun Shourie (2003), a seasoned journalist and ex-cabinet minister of Government

Table 10.2   Export Performance for theYear 2007: Some Select Companies (in US$ Billion)

	Companies	Sales	Export	Export/Sales as %
1.	RIL	26	13	49
2.	Mangalore Refinery	7	2.5	36
3.	Tata Steel	4.3	0.43	10
4.	L&T	4.2	0.83	21
5.	TCS	3.3	3.0	92
6.	Wipro	3.0	2.0	69
7.	Infosys	2.9	2.6	92
8.	Sterlite	2.8	1.6	58
9.	Adani	2.2	0.7	35
10.	HZL	2.0	0.9	45
11.	Suzlon Eng	1.19	0.4	33
12.	Jindal Steel	1.16	0.5	42
13.	Bhushan Steel	0.92	0.3	36
14.	Bharat Forge	0.45	0.2	38

Source: CMIE Prowess Database.

of India, to publish a series of three articles in August 2003. Praising the performance, Shourie was keen to claim that India has arrived. Some examples of this optimism are as follows:

- Twenty to twenty-five years ago, or even 10 years ago, few Indians had heard of Information Technology. Today, exports from this industry are worth $10 billion. This is 20 per cent of our total exports. Infosys was not even been born 25 years ago. Wipro was a company selling vegetable oil. Indeed, other than the Tata Consultancy Services, there was scarcely a name in the IT industry that was known then.
- Fifteen of the world's major automobile manufacturers are now obtaining components from Indian firms. In 2002, exports of auto-components were $375 million. This year they are close to $1.5 billion. Estimates indicate they will reach $15 billion within six to seven years.
- Bharat Forge has the world's largest single-location forging facility of 0.12 million tons per annum. Its client list includes Toyota, Honda, Volvo, Cummins and Daimler Chrysler.
- Essel Propack is the world's largest laminated tube manufacturer. It has a manufacturing presence in 11 countries including China. It has global manufacturing share of 25 per cent, and caters to all of P&G's laminated tube requirements in the US, and 40 per cent of Unilever's (Shourie 2003).

So all put together, the Indian tiger which was caged till 1991 finally got uncaged ('India is a tiger caged': the metaphor of a hard hitting article in *The Economist* [Crook 1991]). Seemingly the 'Indian elephant' of Jim Rohwer (1995), is now moving at a tiger's speed. It is a very positive achievement for a nation which was declared as world's biggest underachiever by *The Economist* (1999). It is true that Indian companies are increasing their global presence but have they become global brands? The answer is No. There is a very long way to go before the Indian giants could claim to be well-known global brands. The latest list of brand values of Interbrand, a London-based brand consultancy firm had not a single brand in its list of top 100 brands from India.

The Image of Brand India

Historically, the 'Made in India' brand has been associated with poor quality and inefficiency (*The Financial Express* 2005). This was true 62 years back and is true even in 2008. Despite the attempts of several Indian companies like Infosys, TCS, Tata Steel, L&T, Bharat Forge and many others, 'Brand India' has a very poor image amongst the global customers, especially from the USA, Europe, Japan and other developed countries. This poor image of 'Brand India' has been a liability for long for several Indian companies.

As early as 1980s, i.e., ever since Tata Steel started its international business, an important sales pitch of Tata's used to be to create a disconnect between India and Tatas. 'We are Tatas and not India!!!' has been the attempt for long. Around late 1996, I happened to be present during a talk by Mr Suresh Krishna, CMD of Sundaram Fastener Limited (SFL), a leader in the field of High Tensile fasteners (nuts and bolts for auto companies) at IIM Bangalore. He shared an interesting experience. This was that even after winning awards like TPM and Deming, General Motors of the USA, before placing order to SFL, even for a low-tech product like radiator caps, set very stringent quality targets. Against the norm of 500 caps, General Motors set a limit of 250 defective caps per million for SFL. But to the credit of SFL, as proudly shared by Suresh Krishna, its first lot of supplies had only 123 defective pieces. The second had only 23 and the third had none. Based on this superlative performance, SFL was rated amongst General Motors' best suppliers. But then, these kinds of sporadic episodes have not helped a great deal in changing the image of India. Baba Kalyani, CEO of Bharat Forge shared that 'it took seven years to find its first customer because coming from so-called underdeveloped low cost country, the company had to battle all kinds of doubts regarding its capability and technology' (Kumar 2009: 88). Similar was the experience of D.S. Brar, CEO and MD of Ranbaxy, when an American company's CEO made him wait for six hours before meeting him (*The Financial Express* 2005).

These were the experiences of the 1990s. As late as 2006, a Director of L&T shared that it took a lot of effort on his part to convince a buyer from New Zealand that L&T is different from other Indian companies. After finishing his week's visit to India, the customer wrote and acknowledged that L&T is definitely not like the other companies of India. He seemingly had a very poor view and experience of dealing with other Indian companies. This poor image of India had adversely affected the image and efforts of even well-known Indian companies. This was in 2006, but the same situation lay even in 2008. Sintex's MD Mr Dangayach shared that in spite of owning the manufacturing firms in Europe and the USA, the foreign auto component manufacturers are still reluctant to give orders to Sintex. He felt that the major barrier is the image of India.

Adding fuel to the fire are the reports that declared India as the 85th most corrupt country in the list of 180 countries in 2008 (Transparancy International 2008). Authors cite the example that it takes two weeks for a truck to reach from Kolkata to Mumbai, a distance of only 2,000 km! Speakers in seminars and news items unhesitatingly mention that the Indian bureaucracy is still being corrupt and inefficient.

The cumulative impact of poor and unreliable image of brand India is the negative rub off on the Indian firms. Thus, even by 2009, in order to practice 'just in time', the auto giants of the US and Europe insisted on the Indian component suppliers to maintain warehouses in their countries. This implies twice the level of inventories. The reason being that the shipping and shipments from India are unreliable. So even when Indian companies have matched the quality gaps, socio-economic infrastructure is still a major weakness. Looking at the Indian ground reality Ramchandran Guha (2009), a famous historian from India shared that infrastructural deficiencies and social ethos would not help India become a super power even by the next 50 years.

The Indian Giants but Global Pygmies

Gupta et al. (2008: 19) in *The Quest for Global Dominance* have shared *The Financial Times* list of the top 500 global giants in terms of Market Cap for the year 2007. This included eight firms each from China and India. Recognizing the emergence of China and India as the two most important markets of global economy, the authors have speculated that by 2025, the list may contain more than 100 firms—in the top 500 list—with headquarters located either in India or China. This is just a speculation. But what matters is the situation now. My study brings out that the gap is very substantial. The global giants make the Indian giants appear as pygmies. Tables 10A.1 and 10A.2 has an illustrative list of the Indian and global giants. A partial glimpse is available in Table 10.3.

Table 10.3 shows that in terms of sale, IBM is 20 times bigger than TCS, GE is 23 times bigger than L&T, Bechtel is five times bigger than L&T and Caterpillar is 52 times bigger than Telcon.

Indian and Global Brands: Why and How the Difference

A strong brand scores high on awareness about its good performance. This creates a positive image and helps in building strong brand equity. This would be true for both local and global brands. The difference is in the scope of awareness about good performance and the image of the brand. So when someone says that brand equity value of Google is 100 billion and that of Infosys is 9 billion (Infosys 2008–09: 131), the difference of 10 times would translate into the level of awareness between the two. Both Google and Infosys are outstanding brands. Infosys, though from India, has nearly 90 per cent of its business from foreign clients. Being essentially an IT service provider—a back-office support function—its visibility is low. Further, being essentially a B2B company, its customer base of 570-plus cannot help it to improve its visibility. So no matter, how hard they try or wish, Infosys's level of global awareness compared to Google would always remain low. (Google gets 200 million click every day [Kotler and Keller 2006: 273].) In India, where it does not to do any significant business, Infosys enjoys excellent brand image cum reputation. Infosys does not advertise like HUL, Airtel or Indica car. It is totally absent on mass media: popular TV channels; print media like daily newspaper or magazines like *India Today*

Table 10.3   Comparison: Indian vs Global Giants

Indian Giants	Year of Inception	Sales (US$ Billion)	No. of Employees	Global Presence (No. of Countries)
IT/Computer Services				
TCS	1968	4.8	143,761	42
Infosys	1981	4.4	103,905	23
Global Giants				
IBM	1911	104	398,455	170
Accenture	1999	25	186,000	53
Engineering/Diversified				
L&T	1946	7	37,000	Offices in 10 locations
				Customers in 30 countries
RIL	1966	35	25,487	–
Global Giants				
GE	1892	183	323,000	62
Bechtel	1898	31	44,000	25
Earth Moving Equipment				
Telcon	1999	0.7	–	–
Global Giants				
Caterpillar	1925	51	112,887	29

(Table 10.3 Continued)

(Table 10.3 Continued)

Indian Giants	Year of Inception	Sales (US$ Billion)	No. of Employees	Global Presence (No. of Countries)
Steel				
Tata Steel*	1907	6	37,205	50
Global Giants				
Arcelor Mittal	2006	125	315,867	60
Thyssen Krupp	1997	80	199,374	36
Nippon Steel	1970	47	50,077	9

Sources: (a) IT/Computer Services

Source for Indian companies: CMIE Prowess; www.tcs.com; www.infosys.com

Source for global companies: Fortune 500 listings available online at http://money.cnn.com/magazines/fortune/global500/2009/; www.ibm.com; www.accenture.com

(b) Engineering/Diversified

Source for Indian companies: CMIE Prowess; http://www.lntecc.com; www.ril.com

Source for global companies: Fortune 500 listings available online at http://money.cnn.com/magazines/fortune/global500/2009/; www.ge.com; www.bechtel.com

(c) Earth Moving Equipment

Source for Indian companies: CMIE Prowess; www.telcon.co.in

Source for global companies: Fortune 500 listings available online at http://money.cnn.com/magazines/fortune/global500/2009/; www.cat.com

(d) Steel

Source for Indian companies: CMIE Prowess; www.tatasteel.co.in/

Source for global companies: Fortune 500 listings available online at http://money.cnn.com/magazines/fortune/global500/2009/; www.arcelormittal.com/; www.thyssenprupp.com ; www.nsc.co.jp/en/index.html

Notes: All data as of March 2009.

*Does not include Tata Corus.

and many more used for the B2C brands. But in a limited manner, it is on popular business channels like NDTV Profit or CNN IBN. Every second or third day, there is news about Infosys on these channels. Mr Narayana Murthy and Nandan Nilekani are sought after by media. Similar to business channels, other newspapers like *The Economic Times*, *The Times of India* and business magazines like *Business Today* and *Business World* too carry news on Infosys. (These could carry news on the performance about foreign acquisition and others.) Even when the frequency of their news may be low on yearly basis, over a period of time, Infosys and Narayana Murthy have become well known in India. With very little money on direct media advertising, Infosys, over a period of time, has become a strong brand in India. But the same is not true for Infosys in places like the US, the UK, Germany and Japan.

Similar is the situation with other Indian giants like the Tatas, A.V. Birla Group, Reliance Industries and others. Even when their companies may be present in more than 100 countries, neither the companies nor their leaders enjoy the same visibility and awareness outside India. They are nowhere near the likes of Bill Gates (Microsoft) or Jack Welch (ex-CEO, GE). Companies like Microsoft, IBM, Accenture, Intel, HP, Caterpillar, Boeing, ABB, Siemens—most of them being B2B companies—enjoy high global visibility. These companies get covered by popular media not only in their home countries but also wherever they go. They get covered in magazines like *Fortune*, *Forbes* and *The Economist*, as well as in newspapers like *Wall Street Journal* and *The Financial Times*. The local newspapers of Singapore, Dubai, Malaysia, China and India among others carry news about them. Their stories and cases appear in management textbooks, business journals like *Harvard Business Review*, *California Management Review* and in several highly credible academic journals. These have very large global circulation and readership. The management textbooks, mainly from America, are read by millions of the students based all over the globe—the US, Europe, Japan, China, Thailand, Malaysia and several other countries with business schools. Articles in journals like *Harvard Business Review*, *California Business Review*, *Journal of Marketing*, *Journal of Brand Management*, *Academy of Management Review* and others are not only read by researchers, but also by students and managers. In short, they are omnipresent. The companies and CEOs are cited by authors based in their home countries as well as by people around the world.

So one would find Indian authors giving examples of GM, Toyota, P&G, Coke, Bill Gates, Jack Welch, Peter Drucker, Philip Kotler, Mike Porter, C.K. Prahalad and the like. Not only have their companies become well known, their professors and consultants have also become celebrities. Each has become a big global brand sought after by many.

Microsoft and Infosys started business at the same time. But compared to Infosys's 5 billion sales of 2008–09, Microsoft's sales is 50 billion. Compared to Infosys brand equity of US$ 9 billion, Microsoft's is US$ 57 billion (as in 2006). Thanks to computerization, many Indians now know Intel, Microsoft Windows, HP, Apple and IBM.

The house of Tatas started their business in 1867. Except for Siemens (1845) and Lafarge (1833), all others like GE, IBM, GM, Ford, Philips, Toyota, Sony, Hyundai, LG, Honda and Samsung started their business much later than the Tatas and Birlas in India. Tatas and Birlas, in spite of having 30–50 per cent of their sales from their operations abroad, do not enjoy the same status of a global brand, unlike the others. They do not get picked up by the global media to become widely known. To overcome this handicap and become a global brand would remain a major challenge for Indian companies for several decades.

Why Go Global?

With the handicaps of poor global brand image and a yawning gap between the size and resources, does it make any sense for Indian companies to create global brands? The reason is simple: Growth opportunities are beyond India. For long, the Indian markets have been small for each and every product service. Table 10.4 provides a quick comparison. Though the gap between India and the highest consumption would be very substantial, even with the world averages, India has a long way to go.

Table 10.4 India and the World: A Comparison of Consumption Levels (Market Size) (Year 2008)

No.	Product	Per Capita		Total		Times
		India*	World**	India	World	
1.	Steel	43 kg	197 kg	50 MT	1,321 MT	26
2.	Aluminium	0.5 kg	5 kg	1.3 MT	38 MT	29
3.	Cement	135 kg	270 kg	157 MT	1,838 MT	12
4.	Air conditioners (No)	2/100		3 million	80 million	27
5.	TV (No)	46/1,000	76/1,000	5 million	23 million	5
6.	Refrigerators (No)	36/1,000	32/1,000	4 million	10 million	2.5
7.	Plastics	6 kg	25 kg	7 MT	168 MT	24
8.	Rubber	930 gm	14 kg	0.86 MT	22 MT	25
9.	Bottled water	3–4 l	25 l	8 bn litre	280 bn litre	35
10.	Paper	7.25 kg	48 kg	8 MT	322 MT	40
11.	Telephone ownership (No)	8.5/100	117/100	400 million	3,000 million (mobile)	7.5
12.	Automobile (No)	12/1,000	164/1,000	14 million	1,100 million	79
13.	PC (No)	15/1,000	121/1,000	16 million	798 million	50

Sources: (a) http://www.equitymaster.com/research-it/sector-info/aluminium/
(b) http://www.cemnet.com/cs/blogs/icr_editors_blog/archive/2009/05/01/Global-warning-_2D00_-cement-growth-slowdown_3F00_.aspx
(c) http://www.nationmaster.com/graph/tra_mot_veh-transportation-motor-vehicles
(d) http://www.assocham.org/prels/shownews.php?id=1346

(Table 10.4 Continued)

(*Table 10.4 Continued*)

(e) http://www.equitymaster.com/research-it/sector-info/Consprds/consprds-products.html
(f) www.indiachem.in/...IssuesAffectingIndia'sCompetitiveAdvantageinChemical.../MrKGovindarajan.ppt
(g) http://www.isoc.org/oti/articles/0401/rao2.html
(h) http://www.marketresearchworld.net/index.php?option=com_content&task=view&id=2957&Itemid=77
(i) HSIL company report by SKP Securities Ltd
(j) http://graphics8.nytimes.com/packages/flash/business/20080907-metrics-graphic/carto6.3.swf
(k) http://graphics8.nytimes.com/packages/flash/business/20080907-metrics-graphic/carto6.3.swf
(l) http://www.rncos.com/Press_Releases/UAEs-Steel-Consumption-to-Reach-15-Million-Tons-by-2012.htm
(m) http://www.blonnet.com/2004/08/17/stories/2004081700620400.htm
(n) news/newsdetails.aspx?news_id=82174&page=2
(o) http://www.europeanplasticsnews.com/subscriber/headlines2.html?cat=1&id=1269338643

Notes: Population (for 2009): *India—1.17 billion; **World—6.80 billion.

Due to low consumption levels China and India would be the major drivers of the global economy. The 21st century has been declared as the century of India and China (Brazil, Russia, India and China [BRICs]). This implies that most of the global brands (both B2B and B2C) would like to become dominant players in China and India. Global competitiveness alone would save the Indian companies. Though China has already become the largest market for products like automobile, steel, cement, air conditioners, cell phones and many more, the Indian markets would remain small for next 10–15 years (*The Financial Express* 2004). The Indian reality dictates that the Indian firms cannot grow unless they aspire to become both global brands and global giants. This should be their aspiration. The efforts of giants would help nearly 0.25 million exporters (as of 2008) from India. Strong brand from a country like India can help in transforming the image of even 'brand India'. This would help both B2B and B2C brands in the global arena. Several Indian companies aware of these challenges and are gearing up to become global brands. In the corporate branding chapters of the house of Tatas, L&T and Infosys, I had discussed the efforts made by these three Indian giants to become global brands. Likewise, there is a long list of other companies like A.V. Birla Group, Vedanta Group, Bharat Forge, Mahindra and Mahindra and many more who are continuously enhancing their global presence and dominance.

Becoming Global Brands: A Major Challenge—Attracting the Talent

A study of Indian scenario suggests several strategies which Indian companies are pursuing. By and large, these can be divided into:

- Set up manufacturing facilities either through acquisition or greenfield routes.
- Open offices and manage the exports from India.
- Set up offices to provide full services to the local clients.
- Continue to do the export business through foreign agents.

Though there are several challenges, which any firm would face when going global, attracting and retaining the desired local talent would be the most difficult challenge. A strong global brand is able to attract the local talent with ease. But this is not the situation for the Indian companies. Thus, whereas companies like IBM, Accenture, GE, ABB, Microsoft, Citi Bank, HSBC, McKinsey, Boston Consultancy, and so on, are sought after companies even in India by the students and prospective employees, the same is not the case even for large Indian companies. The reason is straightforward: The foreign MNCs are strong brands even in India.

So if even in India our giants suffer from this handicap; attracting local talent in the host countries would be a very difficult proposition. At the same time, to become a global brand, a company needs to have global talent. To attract local talent, the Indian companies have to become strong global brand. This is like a Catch-22 situation. Breaking the spiral too would be a major challenge. Development of communication campaigns, participation in trade fairs and acquiring existing ongoing units, to my mind, would be less challenging than the ability to attract and retain local talent. Perhaps attempts of the giants like the house of Tatas, Infosys, Birlas, Bharat Forge and others would help a great deal.

Model of Resource Leveraging: Can It Help India's Brands?

So far whatever I have shared, seems to indicate that creation of a global brand is a daunting task. Should the view be that pessimistic? Answer is No. May be part of the answer lies in the suggestion of Prahalad and Hamel. In their article, 'Strategic Intent', they suggested a resource leveraging model for resource starved firms. Analysing Japanese companies' success, the authors stated:

> In 1970, few Japanese companies possessed the resource base, manufacturing volume, or technical prowess of US and European industry leaders. Komatsu was less than 35% as large as caterpillar (measured by sales) was scarcely represented outside Japan and relied on just one product line-small

bulldozers—for most of its revenue. Honda was smaller than American Motors and looked pitifully as small compared to $4 billion Xerox. Yet by 1985, Komatsu began a global brand with a wide product range of earth moving equipment. Honda was manufacturing as many cars worldwide in 1987 as number three US company Chrysler. Canon's global share had equaled that of Xerox. (Prahalad and Hamel 1989: 2)

Within 20 years the Japanese companies could achieve what seemingly was beyond their resources and capabilities. According to Prahalad and Hamel the Japanese could do it as they had quest for global leadership. They termed this aspiration as 'Strategic Intent'. Could mere articulation of 'Strategic Intent' be a magic wand for the Indian companies to become global brands? The answer needs debating as in spite of the small sizes, the context of Japanese firms, even in the late 1950s and early 1960s, was altogether different from that of the Indian firms even by 2008. The Japanese business environment was very conducive for its firms. The same is not true for Indian firms.

Acquisiton to Accelerate the Learning

Can Indian companies create brands like the Japanese counterparts, especially when many from India feel that 'India and Indian companies do not have culture of creating brand' (Berley 2005). Is creation of global brands lack of imagination or something more than the mere articulation of audacious ambitions? Perhaps both would be needed. Rama Bijapurkar (2005), a revered brand consultant of India, feels that Indian companies need to accelerate their learning for building global brands. According to her the two learnings that Indian companies need are: One, how to gain market access up to the stage of end customers, i.e., beyond B2B situations and two, to find innovative ways to reduce the enormous cost of conventional brand-building communication. To identify low cost, yet impactful communication vehicles, would be a challenge. A feel of the enormous cost of Indian and global media is available in Table 10.5.

Table 10.5   Cost of Media (Year 2009)

S. No.	Publisher	Rate		Specification
Indian Media				
1.	India Today	Rs 340,000	US$ 7,000	per page
2.	Business Today	Rs 190,000	US$ 4,000	per page
3.	Business World	Rs 235,000	US$ 5,000	per page
4.	Business India	Rs 200,000	US$ 4,000	per page
5.	Economic Times	Rs 3,730	US$ 78	per sq cm
Global Media				
1.	CNN	US$ 190,000 (30 Sec)	Rs 9.26 million	
2.	ABC	US$ 125,000 (30 Sec)	Rs 6.1 million	
3.	Economist	£ 21,900	Rs 1,759,731 for half page black and white	
		£ 109,250		
		£ 1,759,173	Rs 8,775,784 for inside front cover	
4.	Wall Street	US$ 62,500	Rs 3 million for one-fourth page black and white	

Sources: For Indian Media the source is Company data.
For global media the sources are:

> (a) CNN Advertise, available online at http://edition.cnn.com/services/advertise/specs/specs_overview.html
> (b) ABC ad rates, available online at http://www.reuters.com/article/idUSTRE61R2YD20100301
> (c) *The Economist*, 'The World in 2009, £ Advertising Rates', available online at www.ads.economist.com
> (d) The *Wall Street Journal* ad rate, available online at http://wsjmediakit.com/magazine/rates/

According to her, in order to accelerate this learning Indian companies should acquire strong brand company of an appropriate size that is preferably global or at least strong in one major geography—like the US or West Europe. Once this happens, rest would follow, feels Rama.

Summing Up: Creating Global Brands—It would be a Long Journey

There is no doubt that acquisition can accelerate the learning for global branding. But can it shorten the time to become well-known global brands? The gap between global leaders and Indian players is very wide and resources very limited. Acquisition and resource leveraging can help in a very limited way. 'Brand building is not magic. It takes decades of globalized environment to become well known global brands. Inspite of all their efforts, Japanese and Koreans could only build limited number of brands like Honda, Toyota, Samsung, Hyundai, Sony, Panasonic, L.G. Hyundai' (Khanna 2005). Based on these examples, many may feel that Indian firms still have a long way to go. But in spite of this some feel that the basic building blocks are in place to create global brands from India. These are liberalized policies due to which Indian companies are increasing their global presence through more and more share in sales from global operations. The other development is the articulation of aspirations like TCS to become the 10th IT service provider by 2010, or Mahindra's desire to become the largest tractor brand of the world. Through these examples, Ajay Khanna, CEO of India Brand Equity Funds, is sensing a new confidence and capabilities in Indian companies to build strong brands. But to my mind achieving global awareness and recognition is still a very long journey. The example of L&T is an illustration. (Readers may also refer to the globalization attempts of House of Tata [Chapter 4] and Infosys [Chapter 6].)

Globalization: The L&T Way

L&T, the engineering giant from India, began its attempts to globalize by setting up exports department around the late 1970s. The destinations were nearby Gulf countries. In 1976, ECC, its construction division, won a contract to build the Abu Dhabi International Aitrport. Over the years ECC has built hotels and housing complexes in Russia. It has built two world-class hotels in Uzbekistan. But in spite of this performance, ECC did not have any permanent set-up anywhere outside it. It never thought of becoming a global contracting firm. ECC's first joint venture firm, L&T Oman, was created in 1993, i.e., nearly 20 years after its export operations. But now it is accelerating the pace of globalization. Currently, ECC has around 700 staff posted in GCC countries. ECC has now created L&T Saudi Arabia. The main concentration will now be in the Middle East with bases in Abu Dhabi and Dubai. Besides these it is also strengthening operations in Tanzania, Kenya, Sudan, Malaysia and Mauritius. By pushing globalization it is trying to achieve 30 per cent of total revenue from global operations. ECC's target for Middle East has been raised from Rs 1 billion to Rs 2 billion sales in the next five years.

In spite of such substantial presence, the Director-in-Charge of ECC shared: 'Till 2008, in spite of being very big in India, ECC was not a strong brand outside India.'

Another division of L&T, Switchgear, with 50 per cent plus market shares in India, still offers a heavy discount to get business from the foreign customers in India and abroad. Though over the years, the discount is coming down, indicating an improvement in L&T's image amongst its foreign customers, but the Director-in-Charge felt that it would not be easy to dethrone the likes of Siemens and Alstom outside India. As part of globalization, L&T's Switchgear has factories in China and in Saudi Arabia. All put together, L&T's global presence is on the rise. Hopefully one day its dream of becoming a 'Bechtel' or 'Flour Daniel' would materialize. But it is still a long way. Similarly through acquisition of Corus after 100 years of its existence, Tata Steel has now become the sixth largest player in the world. But has it become a big global brand? To my mind this is only the first step of a long journey to become a global brand. The same would be true for many Indian brands.

Annexure

Table 10A.1　The Indian Giants and Global Presence (in US$ Billion, 2009)

Name of the Company	Sales[a]	Assets[a]	No. of International Countries in which the Company has Branches[b]	Total No. of Employees[a,b]
Tata group	71	24*	80	357,000
RIL	35	37	16	25,487
Tata Steel-India	6	12	50	34,918
TCS	4.8	3	42	143,761
Wipro	4.7	3.6	31	95,000
Infosys	4.4	3	8	103,905
Grasim	4	4.3	25	13,492
L&T	2	10	9	37,000
HCL	2	2	19	60,000
Bharat Forge	0.4	0.7	6	7,000

Sources:　[a] The data pertaining to sales, assets and total number of employees have been derived from CMIE: Prowess Database; Prowess is a database of large and medium Indian firms. It contains detailed information on over 23,000 firms.
[b] The data pertaining to number of international buyers in which the company has branches and total number of employees have been derived from the following company websites:

　　www.tata.com　　　www.infosys.com
　　www.ril.com　　　　www.grasim.com
　　www.tatasteel.com　　www.larsentoubro.com
　　www.tcs.com　　　　www.hcl.in
　　www.wipro.in　　　　www.bharatforge.com

Note:　*Tata group without Corus.

Table 10A.2   The Global Giants: International Performance (in US$ Billion, 2009)

Name of the Company	Sales[a]	Assets[a]	No. of International Countries in which the company has Branches[c]	Total No. of Employees[a, c]	Brand Value*[b]
Toyota	204	294	143	320,808	34
GE	183	798	62	323,000	53
Arcelor Mittal	125	133	60	315,867	–
Siemens	124	133	98	420,800	8
HP	118	113	170	321,000	23
Samsung	110	83	62	164,600	18
IBM	104	109	170	398,455	59
Nestlé	102	100	Almost all countries	283,000	6
Metro	101	47	32	254,457	–
Hitachi	99	95	41	400,129	–
LG	82	51	51	177,000	–
ThyssenKrupp	80	58	36	199,374	–
Matshushita (now Panasonic)	78	65	58	292,250	4

Sony	77	122	148	171,300	13
Nokia	74	55	128	125,829	36
Hyundai	72	82	180	110,704	5
Bosch	64	–	60	280,000	–
Dell	61	26	172	77,700	12
Mitsubishi	61	111	77	60,095	–
Microsoft	60	73	110	91,000	59
Caterpillar	51	68	23	112,887	5
Intel	38	51	57	83,900	31
Phillips	37	–	100	121,398	8
ABB	35	33	128	125,829	–
Accenture	25	12	53	186,000	8
Haier	17	–	21	50,000	12

Sources: [a] Fortune Global 500, 2009
[b] Interbrand 2008
[c] Company websites and annual reports:

www.toyota.com	www.ibm.com	www.sony.net
www.ge.com	www.nestle.com	www.nokia.com
www.arcelormittal.com	www.metrogroup.de	www.hyundai.com
www.siemens.com	www.hitachi.com	www.bosch.com
www.hp.com	www.thyssenkrupp.com	www.dell.com
www.samsung.com	www.panasonic.net	www.mitsubishi-motors.com

www.microsoft.com
www.cat.com
www.intel.com
www.phillips.com
www.abb.com

Note: *Interbrand valuations.

Table 10A.3   Countries Owning First Hundred Brand in Interbrand Study (2008)

Country	No. of Companies
United States	52
Germany	10
France	8
Japan	7
Switzerland	5
Italy	4
Netherlands	3
United Kingdom	3
Canada	2
Sweden	2
Korea	2
Spain	1
Finland	1

Source: Table made on the basis of the information available in interbrand's report on best global brands; 2008 rankings. See http://www.interbrand.com/best_global_brands. aspx?year=2008&type=asc&col=4&langid=1000

11

The difference between what we do and what we are capable of doing would suffice to, solve most of the world's problems.

—Mahatma Gandhi

～～ ～～

Become your own light.

—Mahavir

11

Rekindling Their Aspirations through the Idea of Brands

Strong Brand as the Aspiration

> Aspiration is the main fuel for progress. Aspirations transform a set of ordinary people into extraordinary achiever.
>
> —Narayana Murthy (Infosys 2005–06: 3)

This quote of Narayana Murthy, Chairman, Infosys, sums up one of the key purposes of this book. Could the idea of 'brand' help the unknown millions to become bigger and widely known? This is an important concern of the book written especially for the B2B marketers. Every second author cites GE, Dupont, Intel, IBM, Microsoft, HP and alike as strong B2B brands (Kotler and Keller 2006). Similarly, in India, Tata Steel, L&T, Infosys, TCS and Reliance Industries are well-known brands in the B2B space. All these were small when they began. Their first step must have been as small or big as the first step of the millions of unknown entrepreneurs. But over a period of time, while a handful have become giants and well known in India, the others have got lost in their own world. They may still be performing well in their chosen businesses. They may also be leaders with dominant market share in their niches. Yet they would be known only to their limited stakeholders. They are neither Indian nor global giants. They may argue that they are very satisfied with their performance and so leave them as they are. They may share several good reasons about their small size and low visibility amongst the common public. All these would be justifiable and valid. But I want to provoke and motivate these millions of companies who are currently cocooned in their own world to accept the challenge to become big and be admired by a large base of the stake holders If few firms from the past can become global giants of today, then why cannot the unknown millions achieve the same? And it is my belief that brand as an idea provides both: inspiration and aspirations. The idea of building brand should be 'a way of life' which can drive the entire business. Brand should be seen a strategic resource which could be leveraged to make organizations visible, vibrant and evergreen.

The Unknown and Unsung Heroes

In the last 40 years, I have come across several entrepreneurs who are still performing well and enjoying a very comfortable, contented and respectful life. But they, even after 40 years of being in business, are part of what I have labelled as the unknown millions. All belong to the domain of B2B and marketing. One is Krishna Kumar (KK) who was from a family with a business history of more than 50 years; he began his independent business career in 1972. His first venture was Megha Limited (name disguised). This was in collaboration with a Swedish firm in the business of rubber liner and other products related to mining and bulk material handling for industries like iron ore, copper ore, steel plants and copper smelting plant. By the end of 2008, K.K. Group had several companies under its fold. The group's sales turnover was around Rs 1,200 million (US$ 25 million). It had manufacturing units in Kolkata and Gurgaon. It employed more than 100 engineers and around 600 workers. In spite of being the leader, and enjoying more than 70 per cent market share for most of his products, Kumar faces perpetual problems of getting and retaining the right human resources. He scores high in source credibility, enjoys a good reputation with his bankers, provides very benevolent salary and perks to his employees, but he is not the first choice by fresh engineers even from lesser known colleges. Even after great difficulties in hiring the engineers and mangers at all levels, the iteration rate is more than 20 per cent per year. He believes in spending lavishly on training, both within and outside, and in spite of hiring many management consultants, he in last 50 years could not cross Rs 1,200 million (in 2008) in sales.

Another entrepreneur who began his business in 1974, as a distributor of pesticides, has now become a mid-size exporter of industrial and leather goods with a sales turnover of around Rs 800 million (US$ 16 million). He would have a team of around 100 people. He is active in his leather export council. His company is not listed and unlike Kumar, he has never hired any professional, either MBA or BBA, from business schools. Whenever I meet him, he is bubbling with ideas to multiply entrepreneurs and innovative ideas for corporate social responsibility. Though he is well known in his business circles, it seems that he would continue to remain a small businessman leading a comfortable life.

The third case is of a salesman converted in to a mid-size trading and manufacturing organization. He has manufacturing units for earth moving equipments and also for the industrial valves. His group's turnover by 2008 was around Rs 1,000 million (US$ 20 million). He too must be employing more than 100 engineers and 700 staff members in his manufacturing and trading and service units. He has plush offices. His staff is smart and well groomed. His promotion material appears world class. He has not left any point of creating visibility and impact untouched. Yet retaining people has been his key problem. In spite of seeking ideas and collaborations from MNCs, his share of business for majority of his products is nowhere compared to the leaders. His dream was to become a big and respected business house in 25 years. But even after 40 years he is nowhere even to figure in the list of top 1,000 companies in India. Till date his companies are not even listed in any of the stock exchanges of India. He identified all the good opportunities for an emerging market like in India. But the absence of focus finally landed him nowhere. His story of entrepreneurship could be best summed up as great ideas with poor implementation.

The fourth in the list is a large chemicals distributor with more than Rs 2,300 million (US$ 46 million) sales. He would be employing more than 300 sales people, He would be amongst the most sought after distributor by leading chemical manufactures of India and the globe. By 2008, he must be representing 80-odd manufacturers.

As I had discussed earlier, they are doing well. But none, at least in their present way of doing their businesses, could claim to be the future house of Tatas, L&Ts, Reliance Industries or Infosys even in the next 25 years. A radical change of their corporate DNA would perhaps be needed to accelerate their transformation. Like these, would be the situation of 2 million plus registered SMEs of India, who are hidden in their cubby holes of multistoried buildings or running their factories in the so-called industrial areas of their cities. Can the idea of becoming a strong corporate brand help them in becoming bigger, better and evergreen? I would like them to carry this belief.

Changing the DNA

The story of these four cases would also be similar to the 600-odd SMEs of Jamshedpur. Jamshedpur, in India, is essentially a B2B city. It is the first steel town of India, established in 1907. Over the years, it has several large-, medium-, small- and tiny-sector organizations. The township belongs to the most respected business house of India: the house of Tatas. Tata Steel, its flagship company, is located in Jamshedpur. Besides Tata Steel, it has Tata Motors, Tinplate Company of India Limited, Tata Robin's Fraser, Telcon, Tata Rolls Limited and UMI. Each company is a leader in its own field. Except for Tata Motors and to a certain extent Tata Steel (both are in B2B and B2C markets), are hardcore B2B companies. A casual inquiry as to how many SMEs would have their websites, the estimates varied from 30 to 60. This, when the cost of developing a website is not even Rs 1,000–2,000 per page and the maintenance cost may not be more than Rs 6,000 per year, shocked me a great deal. This neglect or ignorance reflects that these entrepreneurs have not even thought of laying the seed for building a brand for their organizations. If the seed is missing how can one expect a giant tree tomorrow? You have to make an attempt to differentiate yourself. You would get noticed only if you are different. No one is going to remember you or care about you unless you make an attempt to be different. And if you do not make an attempt, you would remain an unknown entity lost amongst millions.

Big or small, all companies can attempt to create a 'brand' in tune with their philosophy and orientation. This gets reflected when you raise the following question: What do we stand for? This gets reflected when entrepreneurs make an attempt to discover the soul of the organization (Bedbury 2002: 28) and make a new beginning. It is still not late to think of their company as Brand Tata, Brand Infosys and Brand L&T.

What You Stand For: The Starting Point of Brand Building

When Infosys began in 1981, the group of eight promoters debated to what they were chasing. Wwere they chasing money, size or profits? But after a long debate, they stated only one goal for Infosys as a business organization. This was to 'Chase Respect'. Since then, it has remained the guiding principal of Infosys. Since then, it has become the sole rallying point of building the 'brand Infosys'. As shared by Aditya Jha, AVP, Corporate Marketing for Infosys, in a personal interview with the author: 'Brand reflects the soul of an organization. It does not change—no matter what changes around. It is this articulation of soul which then creates several challenges and actions to keep on nurturing and strengthening the brand.'

Gopalakrishnan, Executive Director, Tata Sons, and the main architect of building the brand Tata observes that when J.N. Tata began, he did not have any brand or brand building in his mind. But over the last 140 years, Tatas have become the most respected brand of India. It has earned a reputation where the brand Tata has become synonymous to trust. Mr Gopalakrishnan describes the essence of brand Tata as Tata equals to 'trust'. This 'trust' has become the soul of brand Tata. Today, the brand-building efforts worth US$ 65 billion (in 2008) of the house of Tatas and its 106 companies is to ensure that this trust is not eroded (Agrawal 2007).

Sowing the Right Seed

As mentioned earlier, the two Danish engineers, Holck-Larsen and Soren Toubro, first visited India in 1936 as sales and service engineers for their Danish cement plant manufacturer FLSmidth. But within two years, they realized huge opportunities in infrastructure to build India. The promises to customers must be delivered irrespective of commercial implications. This could not have been possible, if they were not in the L&T seed which was sown in 1938 by Larsen and Toubro.

By 2007, L&T had crossed US$ 5 billion in its turnover. It was employing more than 30,000 professionals and workers. It has become the largest private engineering sector organization of India. It is hardcore B2B organization. But all this could have not been possible had L&T and its professionals not been aligned to the seed.

Contrast this situation with ABC (name disguised), an engineering group with its manufacturing base in western India. Though small and product line being almost similar to L&T, ABC's customer base includes well-known companies like Reliance Industries, Indian Oil Corporation, L&T, Fertilizer Corporation, cement companies, Tata Motors, sugar plants, and so on. Its competitors include companies like L&T, Thermax, Hindustan Machine Tools (HMT), Bharat Heavy Electricals, that is, all well-known companies. By 2007, ABC had become a Rs 10,000 million (US$ 200 million) company. In its own right, ABC, which began its journey in the 1960s, seemingly has done well. Like L&T, it also employs professionals, mainly engineers. Its customers are very happy with its performance. But for a common public and major stakeholders like bankers, suppliers, prospective employees, engineering colleges, customers and local communities, brand ABC is nowhere near brand L&T. If we look at their promotional expenditure, ABC, in terms of percent (A/S), may be spending the same amount as L&T. Like L&T, it also participates in several trade shows and exhibitions—both within India and abroad. Its financial performance and growth have been above industry average. The professionals working within ABC enjoy freedom, space and several good facilities as provided by many well-known organizations of India. Its housing colony is neatly maintained and well-kept, reflecting ABC's concern for people. But as shared earlier, ABC does not enjoy the same visibility and image of Tatas, Infosys or L&T of India. To the Chairman and MD of ABC, this comparison may appear as unfair and harsh. However, it would not be difficult to gauge his predicament of ABC not being a strong brand and evoking the same respect and visibility as several other well-known companies. He could argue that a sale of turnover of Rs 10,000 million over the last 50 years is a good performance and that this should have not been possible if ABC was a poor brand. As a reader, the majority may also endorse his views. On the other hand, a few readers may raise the question as to why ABC could not become as big and visible as Infosys or L&T. Is it because its seeds did not have any explicit statement of what we want to become; in such case what brand would ABC stand for? It is argued that if ABC had also thought of these aspirations in their formative phases, the trajectory of its journey, which otherwise has been successful, could have been different and better. The difference could have enabled ABC to become like L&T, Infosys and even house of Tatas.

Branding Initiatives: Garnering the Power of Convergence and Harmonization

For majority of marketers, 'performance' is the key ingredient of a powerful brand. This is true for both B2C and B2B brands. Minus the performance, no brand can survive. Unlike the product brands of B2C, the majority of B2B players can be classified as Corporate Brands. Consistency in performance over a period of time provides sustenance. In absence of any individual brands, their organization is the brand for their customers. But if you wish to be 'different' for your stakeholders—customers, suppliers, investors, promoters, employees, distribution channel and society at large—then mere product performance would not help you to cast a distinct image of your company to the stakeholders. Even when you are small, not known and are in the business of commodity kind of situation, that is, you are dealing with undifferential product or service, you must make an attempt to create distinctive identity for your business. The brand-buildings efforts (that is, brand activation or branding activities) can help you acquire this image. What I am suggesting is to make a wise and thoughtful use of small spends. Over a period of time, these 'small spends' would make an impact similar to small drops making an ocean. These small spends could be in form of visiting cards, stationary, office decors, dress of employees, colour schemes, logo, office furniture, the receptionist desk, the giveaways like new year gifts, diaries and calendars or website, or even participation in exhibitions and trade shows. Though ultimately your product performance would get you the market share and loyalty, branding efforts can help you acquire a distinct image. I am suggesting what Hague and Jackson (1994: xii) have suggested: 'However, with a little extra effort and cost, the effect could be much improved loyalty and greater profitability.'

Around the early 1990s, I was conducting a 'customer satisfaction cum feedback' study for a ball-bearing manufacturing company. Ball bearings have several end uses. The customers include OEM like auto, fans, pumps, and so on. Bearings being consumables also need replacements. So, the after-market, that is, replacement-market is served by retail channel. This company had both OE and retail markets.

Besides commanding a respect for quality of its products, bearing manufacturers also enjoyed tremendous respect as a very trustworthy company. The feedback study indicated a high customer satisfaction on the quality of bearings. Both the OE and channel were very appreciative of the quality of the product.

What however surprised me, and which was included in the customer satisfaction report, was the almost un-thoughtful and shabby presentation of 'packaging', labels, point of purchase (POP) material, glow signs and billboards for the company. The glow signs for retailers were not standardized. There was no uniformity in the use of colours, letter size, font size of the boards, and so on.

Individually, some appeared very good but all lacked cohesiveness in creating a meaningful impact. In fact, the best and largest board was of a dealer based in Patna (Bihar). I learnt he was a poor performer. Out of curiosity I asked as to how he has such a good sign board. His reply was: I had designed it!

The same study took me to the retail outlets of SKF bearings in several cities. What I recall is the 100 per cent uniform presentation on SKF stockists throughout India. SKF, in India, has always commanded an image of high quality bearings. In its chosen segment it has maintained its leadership for several decades. Due to superior quality, SKF commanded price premium of 5–10 per cent on its bearings. So what additional thing did SKF achieve by having a uniformity in presentation throughout India? One can argue that high quality of bearings commanded loyalty and premium and hence an extra effort for a uniform presentation could not bring in extra premium. In this sense, it is a waste of effort for channel members. Some readers can argue that SKF has stifled creativity and practiced autocracy. By allowing freedom, SKF could have inculcated creativity and imagination of channel members. But to many brand pundits, what SKF is following is the basics of branding and brand management. The practice of this bearing company (for which I was conducting the study) were in contrast to SKF. Did this company lack competency, knowledge and resources? The answer is No. What it did lack was 'thought' and 'thinking' needed to use communication elements (packaging, logos, glow signs, POP material, and so on) to build brands.

Around the mid-1980s, I used to invite the international manager of a leading engineering company as guest speaker for the globalization sessions. In his talk, he would quote his foreign buyers who would say 'your product quality is excellent, but please improve your product presentation'. This was reflective of the poor packaging and identification labels used for these packages. He would feel frustrated that in spite of huge investments to produce world-class products, the Indian companies could never appreciate the importance of brand building by improving product presentation. If they wanted, they could also have thought of providing world-class product presentations. It is being argued that if his company had thought of building strong brands, it could have incorporated all the elements needed to build brands right from the beginning.

Another favourite example which I share from several platforms of various seminars on B2B brands, is that of L&T and many other companies who have a fleet of buses for their employees. If someone conducts a quick recall test as to what is the colour of the fleet buses of L&T, my guess is that nearly 90 per cent would have no problem to answer 'golden yellow'. But the same set of respondents, to my mind, would be confused to recall the colour of buses for other companies. To be sure, it is not uniform for most of the companies. Perhaps other organizations do not see any payoffs from these moving billboards to create corporate image and awareness. May be 'bus' is too trivial a promotional element to develop or create a corporate brand. However, L&T has standardized on golden yellow for all its signages, be it a board for ECC at its construction sites, the trucks carrying ready mix concrete (RMC) or the earth moving equipments made by L&T. All put together, reflects consistency in the thinking of L&T towards brand building. Perhaps the two promoters from Denmark, Larsen and Toubro, sowed the seeds rather early when they developed L&T's logo and standardized on the colour. Today, I am not sure whether it was a chance, a forced decision to standardize on golden yellow, but to an outsider like me, it does reflect a consistent and uniform thinking on part of L&T. There is a thick book of do's and don'ts and of specifications regarding the size and slant of the letters 'L', '&' and 'T' for the logo alone. Besides the guidelines for its logo, L&T has a rule book to guide the branding initiatives of its 75 division.

Like L&T's superb leveraging of its signage, OTIS and Sintex also stand out as excellent examples of enhancing products and company visibility by not spending an additional penny.

It is now more than 40 years, that I started noticing brand-building practices of Indian marketers. What stands out distinctly from my memory are the construction sites with a board of 'OTIS'. The board and the name were sufficient to enhance OTIS's visibility. Contrast to this, I do not remember seeing such boards of OTIS's competitors. Either I do not know them or they are too shy to announce their presence!

Like OTIS, a company which seemingly unleashed a mind-blowing power of brand visibility is Sintex water tanks. 'Sintex', written in white on black tanks, sitting on top of millions of buildings in India, to my mind has no other parallel example of product visibility from India. Sintex is essentially a B2B product. 'Sintex on Top' is my favourite phrase to describe both the reality of tanks sitting on top of the buildings and Sintex as a company enjoying the largest market share—almost 50 per cent for water tanks. And Sintex has achieved this national visibility by spending a very low amount of 0.4–0.5 per cent of sales on promotion and advertising.

Summing Up

Brand as a way of life—It is all in the mind

How do you look at brands and branding in the B2B context would ultimately make the difference in your brand-building efforts and finally in your dreams, vision and strategic plan. With small spends and a narrow customer base, you may argue that nothing else but performance would help. You may, therefore, remain indifferent to reap payoffs through branding. But if you feel that 'brand' is the ultimate of all your efforts, then your approach to manage your brand and business would be different. It would then force you to think about holistic brand management (Kotler and Pfoertsch 2006: 15). I fully endorse what Aditya Jha, AVP, Corporate Marketing, Infosys shared with me:

> Every organization can build around brand. It is their choice—the key thing is firm's ability to walk the talk. You should be able to deliver on your promise. What is important is to know what you stand for—this then becomes the guide post for all your decisions. It does not matter whether you sell chocolates, creams or cranes.

According to him 'brand management has to be an understanding of all the delivery mechanism. Every single aspect of organization affects the brand.' Brand in this sense becomes everybody's business. It then goes way beyond, what marketing does or even does not know. It is not an affair limited to the marketing or corporate communications department. This is almost similar to the suggestions of Scott Bedbury (2002: xiv) where he observes: 'Building and supporting a great brand is everyone's job, from CEO and down.'

12

Imagination is more important than knowledge.

—Albert Einstein

〰〰 〰〰

A great brand is a story that is never completely told.

—Scott Bedbury

12

Reflections and Afterthoughts

During the course of writing this book, I read several books, hundreds of articles and project reports and presentations. I also interacted on one-to-one basis with more than 200 executives. During the course of my research, analysis and writing of drafts, several thoughts came to my mind which I could not cover in the earlier chapters. I wish to share these in the last chapter.

A Shocking Discovery: The Idea of B2B Brands has been Dormant for Decades

I am with XLRI, a top ranking business school for post graduate education (MBA) in India. Since 1976, that is, the time I joined XLRI, I have been offering an elective course in Industrial Marketing (B2B Marketing) to senior students of the Business Management Programme. In the last 34 years, I must have offered this elective course to more than 150 batches in India and abroad. My PhD thesis (in 1990) was in the area of Industrial Marketing Communications. The communications elements include print advertising, trade shows, seminars, hoardings, direct mailers, product and corporate brochures, websites and e-mails and many more. These are also known as branding elements. The bibliography of my thesis contains a list of more than 100 articles, all in the area of brand-building elements. Most of them were first published in the US journals. My thesis also included international comparisons mainly between the UK, the USA and India. It has more than 265 pages and may have more than 130 tables. It was a very rigorous analysis of the management of brand-building elements for B2B markets.

While writing this book, I revisited my thesis. I wanted to borrow those elements which could be relevant for B2B brands. Surprisingly, in the entire thesis, the articles that I referred to or the text that I wrote, there was no mention—even once—of the word 'brand'. Researchers and B2B marketers were neither talking nor practicing the idea of brand and branding then. It was not only my ignorance, but also of the entire set of B2B researchers, scholars and practitioners, who could not sense and see the unexploited and hidden power of leveraging from the concepts of brand and branding. But post 1990, two developments seem to have triggered the interest on B2B brands. One is the widely shared story of 'Intel Inside' since early 1990. The other is that out of world's top 10 brands, five are essentially B2B brands—Microsoft, Intel, GE, IBM and Nokia. Hopefully, the momentum gained would generate more interest in B2B brands. But treatment of majority of authors is still confined to either high-tech IT companies (Aaker and Joachimsthaler 2000: 21) or confined to the hybrid market brands like I Microsof, Intel, and so on (Quelch 2007).

It is my view that interest in B2B brands should not be due to high valuations of a few brands operating in hybrid markets. This should be more to make a case for payoffs by following the concepts of brands for hardcore B2B marketers. This book is one such attempt. Today the disparity in the interest between B2B and B2C brands is glaring. A Google search on 19 November 2009 indicated the availability of some 40 million articles and books when the search command was for all the articles and books on brands. But when the search command was for all articles and books on B2B brands, the number was as low as 58,000.

There seems to be no shortage of brands, concepts, framework and models. Though their utility will remain debatable, current profligacy is so overwhelming that one starts gasping even before one can grasp and comprehend. The information overload coupled with the over usage of jargon has made the beautiful world of brand a jungle of jargons and meaningless frameworks. The authors seem to be in a race to confuse rather than contribute. Larry Bossidy's quote 'Complexity is not the sign of intellectual gift. Making things simple is'[1] and Trout's views 'Complexity is not to be admired. It's to be avoided' (Trout with Rivkin 1999: 8) are excellent reminders for several brand pundits to remain simple and helpful.

Wisdom of Saint Kabir and Understanding the Idea of Brand

Indian literature is rich in providing very deep and profound insights to manage one's affairs in the world. My favourite has been Saint Kabir. His thoughts have had great influence on me. I found two couplets which carry excellent message to the creation and meaning of brand. These are:

Karta tha to kyon kiya, Ab kare kyon pachtaye
Boya ped babool ka, to aam kahan te paye

Dheere dheere re mana, dheere sab kutch hoye
Maali seenche sau ghada, ritu aye phal hoye

The first couplet is a crude reminder to innumerable B2B marketers with weak brands: either of the corporate as a whole or a product. A straightforward meaning of the couplet is: 'You reap what you sow.' A literal translation is:

> When you were doing, you did not question as to what you are doing. Having done what you have done, there is no point repenting on it. When you sowed the seeds of bitter babool tree (Acacia), how can you expect sweet mangoes from that tree.

Kabir's message is simple that it is not a chance which would you give a strong brand, i.e., mangoes, if you in the first place never thought of creating strong brands, i.e., planting and nurturing a mango tree. My interactions with a large majority of B2B marketers reveals that for several years, especially in the formative phase of managing their business, their energies remain confined to managing business for survival. 'Me too' comes out to be the meaning of their identity. There seems to be no attempt to create a distinctive identity for themselves. And when realization dawns, they appear repentant and helpless. The challenges of business are several. But with little thought, one can always attempt to create something different and satisfying.

The second couplet shares that patience is essential in every creation and its process. Drawing an analogy from the gardener, Kabir says that by over-watering, a gardener cannot precipitate the process of bearing fruits for the tree: the tree will bear fruits at the appropriate time. The same is true for brands. As quoted earlier in Chapter 4, Gopalakrishnan, Executive Director, Tata Sons, has a parallel. By putting nine maids and nine doctors, you cannot reduce the time of delivery of the baby from nine months to one month. It takes time to create brands. They cannot be created overnight (Singh 2008).

The Brand Mystique: The Omnibus World of Brands

The most frequently mentioned view about brand is that it is an intangible concept. While discussing various facets of intangibility, several authors have also coined the concepts like brand Dharma, brand Astras (Kapoor 2003). These are well-known terms from Hindu mythology and Sanskrit. A Sanskrit *shloka*, recited by many Indians everyday, appears to be apt to capture the many faceted views on brand. This is:

Tvameva Mata cha Pita Tvameva, Tvameva Bandhu cha Sakha Tvameva,
Tvameva Vidya Dravinam Tvameva, Tvameva Sarwam Mum Dev Deva

You are my Mother and You are my Father; You are my True Relative,
You are the Divine Wisdom, You are the Highest Wealth, You are All in All.

The *shloka* sums up very succinctly the true power of the word, i.e., brand. Today, I find a very wide usage of the term 'brand' to describe the identity of anyone, be it a country—brand India—be it a company—brand Tata Steel—or be it a business school—brand XLRI. This is helpful and powerful way to convey through one word the several intersecting and interdependent decisions and actions impacting brand image and its perception.

Brand and *Raga*: Understanding the Meditative Dimension of Brand

While listening to the discourses on the appreciation of Indian classical music, I came across a wonderful explanation on Indian *raga*s. The speaker was sharing that *raga* has its own meditative meaning. It cannot be created but discovered. The mood of *raga* is not merely playing on the *swara*s, it is living the *swara*s. It has a nostalgic past but it cannot be stored. It cannot be left for future. As the artist plays, the *raga*'s meaning starts unfolding in the present; *raga*s enliven the present and are emotionally and mystically rich. This explanation almost echoes what Bedbury had written for the creation of brands. He had observed: 'Building a brand is the most challenging, complicated and painstaking process that a company can embark on. Its more intuitive than analytical and most of the time it can't be seen. But it can always be felt' (Bedbury 2002: xvi).

In Hindustani classical music every artist plays the same *swara*s (notations) of the *raga* but then the same *raga* from a maestro appears an excellent lilting and lasting experience which lingers forever. For a novice, playing the same *swara*s it appears like cacophony—harsh, un-rhythmic and unbearable. Similar is the situation with the impact of brand. You may have produced your product as per the specification but yet when you deliver to the customer, it is a different experience from each supplier. This is what 'brand' does for thousands of products. With similar specifications, the customer feels that they are different. The difference is of the perception and experiences over the years.

My Simple Model of Creating and Understanding Brand

There is no shortage of brand models. A quick reference to any text can help you know many. However, reflecting upon all that what I have studied and known, the two pillars of creating a strong brand could be 'performance' and 'behaviour'. Figure 12.1 is the conceptualization of this idea. Every B2B organization has to score

Figure 12.1   A Performance and Behaviour Model for Brand Experience

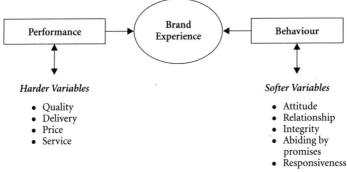

Source: Author.

high on both. It cannot be only one. In this hyper-competitive world, the key differentiators would come when the brand scores very high on ethics and integrity: the softer side of a brand. Humility and humanity (one of the seven core values suggested by Bedbury) would be the traits of a great brand (Bedbury 2002: 188).

It Costs the Same, whether You Dream Big or Small

'Dream big as it costs the same whether you dream big or small.'[2] This is how Nandan Nilekani summed up his remarks for a tutorial being conducted by NDTV Profit: The audience was essentially the young entrepreneur belonging to SMEs.

These words of Nandan Nilekani are most helpful words for all. A great brand starts with a dream. As Dhirubhai of Reliance Industry used to say: 'If you can dream: you can do it.' The problem is that millions of B2B marketers are not even dreaming to become big and create a brand-driven business.

Brand or Not to Brand: The Final Conclusion

After writing this book, I am convinced that brand as an idea is relevant for all. The debate like B2B brands vs B2C brands is irrelevant, meaningless and a waste of time. The principles to create a powerful or a great brand would remain the same, whether you try to create 'brand India', 'brand Infosys' or brand a steel pin. But their context would determine their brand-building challenges. Even without any visibility in the public eye, every B2B organization can attempt to transform itself by creating a brand-driven organization. It is never too late. Attempting to become a brand-driven business can accelerate the process of transformation (Kotler and Pfoertsch 2006: 186).

My good wishes to all B2B marketers.

Notes

Chapter 1

1. I am grateful to A. Ramakrishnan, ex-Dy MD of L&T (ECC), for sharing the episode.

Chapter 3

1. This chapter is based on the personal interviews conducted by the author.
2. One US dollar equivalent to Rs 48 (as on August 2009).

Chapter 4

1. Quotes of J.N. Tata are available online at http/www.tata.com/(downloaded on 26 July 2009).
2. (a) The contribution to sales of 62.55 billion in FY 2008 from various business sectors was:

    (i)   Materials: 52 per cent
    (ii)   Engineering: 17 per cent
    (iii) Information technology: 16 per cent
    (iv)   Services: 4 per cent
    (v)   Chemicals: 3 per cent
    (vi)   Consumer products: 6 per cent
    (vii) Energy: 4 per cent

   (b) The contribution to profit in FY 2008 was:

    (i)   Materials: 56 per cent
    (ii)   IT: 16 per cent
    (iii) Consumer products: 9 per cent
    (iv)   Energy: 5 per cent
    (v)   Services: 3 per cent

3. Available online at http//www.tata.com/media
4. Though thousands of articles are available on the house of Tata and its several organizations, but for a highly readable and insightful familiarity, I would recommend interested reader to read all the books of R.M. Lala. These are: *The Creation of Wealth, The Romance of Tata Steel, For the Love of India.*
5. The quote has been taken from Branzei and Nadkarni (2008).
6. See http//www.tata.com/about us/articles (downloaded on 26 July 2009).

Chapter 5

1. From the CD provided by the Corporate Communication Department of L&T. Most of the quotations of this chapter are based on house magazines and newsletters issued by L&T from time to time till 2009.

Chapter 6

1. Available online at http//www//infosys.com (downloaded on 11 June 2008).
2. US$ 1 = Rs 48 (as of July 2009).
3. As quoted in Narayana Murthy's speech to New York University's Stern School of Business, New York, USA on 9 May 2007. This speech was published in *The Economic Times* later (Narayan Murthy 2007):

   … that in the 17 years since that day [1990], Infosys has grown to revenue in excess of $3.0 billion, a net income of more than $800 million and a market capitalization of more than $28,000 million, 28,000 times richer than the offer of $1 million on that day. As the story goes, Infosys was offered US dollar 1 million in 1990 for which partners were excited to sell it off and lead a comfortable life thereafter. By continuing to own Infosys, it has now created more than 70,000 well paying jobs, 2,000-plus dollar millionaires and 20,000-plus rupee millionaires.

Chapter 7

1. About Jasubhai Group: Indian Architect and Builder (IA&B). Under the aegis of the Jasubhai Media Group and across the last two decades, IA&B has emerged as the country's premier architecture magazine focusing on communicating advances in architecture and design. Its readership profile consists of a cross

section of the country's leading professionals from the AEC (architecture, engineering and construction) industry. The magazine has a readership of approximately 300,000 and has the expertise to deliver quality content over multiple platforms.

Chapter 8

1. Available online at www.netcraft.com/survey (downloaded on 30 January 2010).
2. Available online at en.wikipedia.org/Google_search (downloaded on 16 December 2009).

Chapter 9

1. In the year 2007 Lifebuoy, a brand from HUL, sold more than 100,000 tons of its products. This could be equivalent to hundred million soap cakes of 100 gm each.
2. Available online at http//www.otisworldwide.com (downloaded in January 2010).
3. Available online at http//www.otisworldwide.com (downloaded in January 2010).

Chapter 10

1. World Bank Report, available online at http/www.worldbank.org
2. See Indian Industry Directory of Indian Suppliers, available online at www.indianindustry.com (downloaded on 21 November 2009).
3. See Project Monitor website, http://www.projectmonitor.com

Chapter 12

1. Larry Bossidy, CEO, Allied Signal.
2. Nandan Nilekani, tutorial conducted by NDTV Profit, 28 June 2008.

References

Aaker, David A. 1996. *Building Strong Brands*. New York: The Free Press.

Aaker, David A. and Erich Joachimsthaler. 2000. *Brand Leadership*. New York: The Free Press.

Agrawal, Sujata. 2007. Interview with Gopalakrishnan, 'A Grand Brand'. Interview held in February 2007. Available online at http//www.tata.com/media/interviews. Downloaded on 8 May 2009.

Alexander, Ralph S., James S. Cross and Richard M. Hill. 1967. *Industrial Marketing*. Homewood, Illinois: Richard D. Irwin Inc. Indian edition published by D.B. Taraporevala Sons and Co. Pvt. Ltd (1975).

Ames, B. Charles and James D. Hlavacek. 1984. *Managerial Marketing for Industrial Firms*. New York: Random House Inc.

Anderson, James C. and James A. Narus. 2003. *Business Marketing Management*. New Jersey: Pearson Prentice-Hall.

Ansoff, Igor H. 1965. *Corporate Strategy*. New York: McGraw-Hill Book Company, Inc.

Bansal, Rashmi. 2008. *Stay Hungry, Stay Foolish*. Ahmedabad: IIM Ahmedabad Centre for Innovation, Incubation and Entrepreneurship (CIIE).

Bedbury, Scott. 2002. *A New Brand World*. New York: Viking Penguin.

Berley, Charles. 2005. 'Can India Brands Make Brand India Global?' *The Financial Express*, 20 August.

Bijapurkar, Rama. 2005. 'Can India Inc Build Global Brands?' 8 December 2005. Available online at http/www.rediff.com. Downloaded on 16 September 2009.

Blyth, Alex. 2008. 'Technology: Bringing Your Website Up to Scratch'. Available online at www.b2bm.biz>Features. Downloaded on 30 October 2009.

Brand Finance Global 500. 2009. 'The Annual Report on the World's Most Valuable Brands', April. Available online at www.brandfinance.com. Downloaded on 4 August 2009.

Branzei, Oana and Anant Nadkarni. 2008. 'The Tata Way: Evolving and Executing Sustainable Business Strategies', *Ivey Business Journal*. Available online http://www.iveybusinessjournal.com/article.asp?intArticle_ID=750. Downloaded on 7 July 2009.

Business Week. 2008. 'The World's 50 Most Innovative Companies 2009', Special Report, No. 13, April.

Centre for Monitoring Indian Economy (CME), 2008. Prowess Database. Available online at http.//www.cmie.com
———. 2009. Prowess Database. Available online at http://www.cmie.com.
Chacko, Philip. 2005. 'A Brand Apart'. Available online at http/www.tata.com/article. Downloaded on 20 May 2008.
Chakraborty, G., P. Srivastava and D.L. Warren. 2005. 'Understanding Corporate B2B Web Sites' Effectiveness from North American and European Perspective', *Industrial Marketing Management*, 34(5): 420–24. Available online at www.sciencedirect.com. Downloaded on 20 October 2009.
Crook, Clive. 1991. 'Small World (A Survey of India)', *The Economist*, 4 May.
Dunn, Michael and Scot M. Davis. 2004. 'Creating the Brand-Driven Business: It's the CEO Who Must Lead the Way'. Available online at http://www.prophet.com/downloads/articles/dunn-davis-creating-bdb.pdf. Downloaded on 2 March 2009.
Gandhy, Sherna. 2004. 'From Rehab to Rebirth'. Available online at http://www.tata.com/articles.aspx. Downloaded on 26 July 2009.
Ghoshal, Sumantra, Gupta Piramal and Sudeep Budhiraja. 2001. 'Infosys Technologies Limited: Going Global', in *World Class in India*, pp. 618–39. New Delhi: Penguin Books India.
Gopalakrishnan, R. 2004a. 'Managing Reputation—The Corporate Brand', Presentation at the CII Seminar, Brand Wagon—Branding for Business Success, Jamshedpur, Jharkhand, 10 August.
———. 2004b. 'Scylla and Charybdis: The Business of Business'. Available online at http://www.tata.com/media/Speeches/inside.aspx?artid=O6dLuPys0C0=. Downloaded on 19 November 2009.
Gregory, James R. 2004. *The Best of Branding*. New York: The McGraw-Hill Companies.
Guha, Ramchandran. 2009. 'Superpower Fantasies', *The Telegraph*, Kolkata, 12 September.
Gupta, Anil K., Vijay Govindarajan and Haiyan Wang. 2008. *The Quest for Global Dominance*. New Delhi: John Wiley & Sons, Inc.
Hague, Paul and Peter Jackson. 1994. *The Power of Industrial Brands*. London: McGraw-Hill Book Company.
Hutt, Michael D. and Thomas W. Speh. 2007. *Business Marketing Management: B2B*. Noida: Anubha Printers (First Indian Reprint).
Infosys. 2005–09. *Annual Reports*. Bangalore, India: Infosys.
———. 2008. *Sustainability Report*. Bangalore, India: Infosys.
Irani, J.J. 2008. 'Being a Tata Person', Tata Refractories Limited, Company's House Magazine, Belpahar.
Jagannathan, R. 2002. 'How Tata Steel Made It to Top of the World', *Indian Management*, June, p. 53.
Kapoor, Jagdeep. 2003. *9 Brand Astrus*. New Delhi: Response Books.

Kapston. 2009. 'User Experience/Usability Study'. Available online at www. kapston.com. Downloaded on 8 October 2009.

Keller, K.L. 1998. *Strategic Brand Management*. New Jersey: Pearson Education/ Prentice-Hall.

———. 2005. 'East Watch'. Newletter of CII, Eastern Region. August 2005.

———. 2008. *Strategic Brand Management*. 2nd and 3rd editions. New Jersey: Pearson Education/Prentice-Hall.

Khanna, Ajay. 2005. 'CEO IBEF Can India Inc Build Global Brands?' Available online at http/www.rediff.com. Downloaded on 16 September 2009.

Kotler, P. 2003. *Marketing Management*, 11th Edition. New Jersey: Prentice-Hall.

Kotler, P. and Kevin Lane Keller. 2006. *Marketing Management*, 12th edition. New Jersey: Pearson Prentice-Hall.

Kotler, P. and Waldermar Pfoertsch. 2006. *B2B Brand Management*. Berlin, Heidelberg/New York: Springer.

Kumar, Nirmalya. 2009. *India's Global Powerhouses*. Boston: Harvard Business Press.

Kurian, Boby. 2004. 'Having a Conscience is in Our DNA'. Interview of Nandan Nilekani by Boby Kurian. *Business Line*, Internet editon, 15 April.

Lala, R.M. 1992. *The Creation of Wealth*. Bombay: IBH Publishers.

———. 2004. *For the Love of India*. Bombay: IBH Publishers.

———. 2007. *The Romance of Tata Steel*. Noida: Gopsons Paper Ltd.

Larsen & Toubro (L&T). 2007. *Annual Report*. Mumbai.

Levitt, T. 1967. 'Communications and Industrial Selling', *Journal of Marketing*, 31(April): 15–21.

Lillien, Gary L. 1976. 'Advisor 2: Modeling the Marketing Mix Decision for Industrial Products', *Management Science*, 25(February): 191–304.

Lillien, Gary L. and John D.C. Little. 1976. 'The ADVISOR Project: A Study of Industrial Marketing Budgets', *Sloan Management Review*, 17(3): 17–32.

Madison, Angus. 2003. *The World Economy: Historical Statistics*. Paris: OECD.

Moore, Geoffrey. 2009. 'Why Branding Matters in B2B'. Available online at blog. marketo.com/blog./2007/03/b2b_branding. Downloaded in May 2009.

Mudambi, S.M. 2002. 'Branding Importance in Business-to-Business Markets: Three Buyer Clusters', *Industrial Marketing Management*, 31: 525–33.

Narayana Murthy, N.R. 2005. 'Narayan Murthy's Dream for the Future'. Speech given on 25th Year of Existence, 12 August 2005. Available online at http://www.rediff.com/money/2005/aug/12bspec.htm. Downloaded on 12 September 2009.

———. 2006. Speech at the George Washington University's School of Business for the Annual Robert P. Maxon Lecture, 6 February. Available online at http://www.rediff.com/money/2006/feb/15infy.htm. Downloaded on 16 December 2008.

Narayana Murthy, N.R. 2007. 'Some Lessons from the Life and Career of a Visionary', Speech delivered by Narayana Murthy, Stern School of Business, New York University, New York on 9 May. Published in *The Economic Times*, Chennai, 28 May 2007.

————. 2009. *A Better India, A Better World*. India: Penguin Books India Private Ltd.

Porter, Michael E. 1980. *Competitive Strategy: Techniques for Analyzing Industries and Competitors*. New York: The Free Press.

Prahalad, C.K. and Gary Hamel. 1989. 'Strategic Intent', *Harvard Business Review*, 67(3): 63–67.

————. 1994 *Competing for the Future*. Boston, Massachusetts: Harvard Business School Press.

Quelch, John. 2007. 'How to Build a B2B Brand', Howard Business Publishing online, Posted on 20 November 2007 by Glenn Gow. Available online at http://blogs.hbr.org/quelch/2007/11/how_to_build_a_b2b_brand_1.html. Downloaded on 10 May 2008.

Raghavan, E. and Mitu Jayashankar. 2007. 'Infosys is Now a Smart and Young Lady', *The Economic Times*, 25 October.

Ravikumar, R. 2006. 'Building Brands of Steel', *Business Line*, 31 August 2006. Available online at http://www.thehindubusinessline.com/catalyst/2006/08/31/stories/2006083100160100.htm

Reliance Industries Limited (RIL). 2007–08. *Annual Report of Reliance Industries Limited*, Mumbai.

Report Buyer. 2007. 'Industry Report—India B2B Market Update', March. Available online at http://www.reportbuyer.com/leisure_media/publishing/industry_report_india_b2b_market_update_1.html. Downloaded on 17 October 2009.

Reputation Institute. 2008. *Reputation Institute's 2009 Global Reputation Pulse Report*. Available online at www.slideshare.net/ReputationInstituteESP/2008-global-reputation-pulse. Downloaded on 20 May 2009.

Rohwer, Jim. 1995. *Asia Rising*. London: Nicholas Brealey Publishing.

Roy, Prannoy. 2005. Interview with Prannoy Roy, NDTV, Taj Palace, New Delhi.

Sarin, Sharad. 1990. 'Management of Non-Personnel Communication Efforts for Industrial Marketing: A Study of Indian Firms', Unpublished thesis, Pune University.

Shourie, Arun. 2003. 'Before the Whinning Drowns It Out, Listen to the New India', 15 August; 'When Sky is the Limit', 16 August; 'This is India's Moment but Its only a Moment, Can We Grasp It?' 17 August, *Indian Express*, New Delhi.

Singh, Piya. 2008. 'Eyes on the World', *Business World*, New Delhi, 4 January.

Sintex. 2005–09. *Annual Report*. Ahmedabad.

Tata Steel. 2009. *Annual Report*. Mumbai.

The Economic Times. 1996. 'Tata Brand Holds the High Ground'. Available online at http//www.tata.com. Downloaded by Philip Chacko on December 2003.

The Economic Times. 1999. 'Transformation of World's Biggest Under Achiever Normalising India (India's Future)', *The Economic Times*, 4 September.

The Financial Express. 2004. 'The Essence of the Brics Report', *The Financial Express*, 23 October. Available online at http://www.financialexpress.com/news/the-essence-of-the-brics-report/100328/0. Downloaded on 3 July 2009.

———. 2005. 'Can Indian Brands Make Brand India Global', *The Financial Express*, 20 August. Available online at http://www.financialexpress.com/news/canindianbrandsmakebrandindiaglobal/78211/3. Downloaded on 10 October 2009.

Transparency International. 2008. 'Corruption Perception Index'. Available online at www.rediff.com. Downloaded on 9 May 2009.

Trout, Jack. 2009. 'We're Running Out of Brands'. Available online at http//www.forbes.com/2008/05/09trout-marketing-brands-oped-ex_jt_0509trout,html. Downloaded on 2 July 2009.

Trout, Jack with Steve Rivkin. 1999. *The Power of Simplicity*. New Delhi: Tata McGraw-Hill.

Vitale, Robert and Joseph Giglierano. 2002. *Business to Business Marketing*. Mumbai: Thomson Asia Pvt. Ltd.

Webster, Frederick E. Jr. 1984. *Industrial Marketing*, 2nd edition. New York: Ronald Press Publication, John Wiley & Sons.

Webster, F.E. and Y. Wind. 1972. *Organizational Buying Behaviour, Foundations of Marketing Series*. Engelwood Cliffs, NJ: Prentice-Hall.

Xavier Labour Relations Institute (XLRI). 2003. 'Branding in Industrial Marketing—Case on Buying Centre of Tata Steel', Unpublished report, XLRI, Jamshedpur.

Index

About the Author

Sharad Sarin is Professor of Marketing and Strategic Management, XLRI, Jamshedpur, India. He has been associated with this institution as a faculty member since 1976 and has been the Dean of XLRI from 1984 to 1988. Professor Sarin has been a visiting faculty to the Indian Institute of Management, Ahmedabad, the University of Rhode Island, Kingston, USA, the Colorado University at Boulder, USA and the Helsinki School of Economics, Finland. He was on the Board of XLRI (1993–2004) and Mudra Institute of Communications (1991–2010). Since 2000, he in on the Board of Tata Refractories Ltd.

For the past three decades, Professor Sarin has been involved in several consultancy assignments including marketing studies for a huge number of Indian and overseas companies like Kirloskar Oil Engines Ltd; Elgi Equipments Ltd; Tega Industries; Tata Sponge Iron Ltd; Tinplate Co. Ltd; SAIL; Usha Mrtin Industries; Birla Technical Services; Gujarat Cooperative Milk Marketing Federation Limited (GCMMFL–AMUL); National Dairy Development Board; Grasim Industries; Tata Refractories; Tata Robins Frazer; Tata Steel, Century Textiles, Thailand; Indo Phil Textiles, Philippines; Milliken Carpets, USA; Nigerian Paper Mills, Nigeria; Orind International Limited, China, and so on.

He has also conducted training programmes for senior- and middle-level business executives for his various national and international clients.

His major areas of interest are competition and globalization, corporate planning, general marketing, industrial marketing, marketing's role in development, relationship marketing and strategic marketing.

In November 1995, Sharad Sarin was named amongst the top five teachers of business management in India by *Business Standard*, a leading business daily newspaper in India. He is widely known as the originator of the novel concept of 'Marketing Fair'. From 2001 to 2003, he was on the panel of judges for the Prime Minister's Trophy to select the best integrated steel plant in India.

P306230